Nuremberg

(Germany)

Travel Guide

2025

© *Channah David*

© **2025 Channah David**

All rights reserved. No part of this publication may be reproduced, stored in a retrieval system, or transmitted in any form or by any means—electronic, mechanical, photocopying, recording, or otherwise—without prior written permission from the publisher.

This guide is intended to offer insights, suggestions, and practical tips for exploring **Nuremberg, Germany,** based on personal experiences and general knowledge. While it provides a helpful starting point, it does not encompass every possible experience or location in the area. Readers are encouraged to use it as a foundation, tailoring the information to suit their own preferences and needs. Your personal adventures and discoveries will further enhance the value of this guide.

TABLE OF CONTENTS

Welcome to Nuremberg — 10

Why Nuremberg in 2025? — 13

Chapter 1 — 17

Travel Planning & Essentials — 17

Entry Requirements: Visas, COVID-19 Guidelines & Travel Insurance — 17

Best Time to Visit: Seasons, Weather & Festivals — 20

Language & Cultural Etiquette — 22

Packing List: What to Bring for Every Season — 23

Chapter 2 — 26

Getting to Nuremberg — 26

Arriving by Air: Nuremberg Airport Guide — 26

Traveling by Train: Nuremberg's Rail Connections — 28

Road Trip to Nuremberg: Driving & Parking Tips — 30

Public Transport Overview: Trams, Buses & Bike Rentals — 32

Chapter 3 — 35

Where to Stay in Nuremberg — 35

Luxury Hotels – Iconic 5-Star Accommodations — 35

Mid-Range Comfort – Best Value-for-Money Hotels — 37

Budget-Friendly Stays – Hostels and Affordable Lodging — 38

Unique Stays – Boutique Hotels and Historic Inns — 39

Best Areas to Stay: Old Town vs. Outer Districts — 40

Chapter 4 — 44

Exploring Nuremberg's Old Town (Altstadt)	44
Chapter 5	**57**
Top Attractions in Nuremberg	57
Chapter 6	**66**
Nuremberg's Must-Visit Museums	66
Germanisches Nationalmuseum – The Largest Cultural Museum In Germany	67
Documentation Center Nazi Party Rally Grounds – Understanding History	69
Toy Museum (Spielzeugmuseum) – A Delight For All Ages	72
Memorium Nuremberg Trials – A Legacy Of Justice	74
Db Museum (German Railway Museum) – A Train Lover's Paradise	77
Chapter 7	**80**
Outdoor Activities & Nature Escapes	80
Hiking Trails & Scenic Walks Near Nuremberg	81
Best Parks & Gardens in the City	84
Cycling Routes & Bike Tours	85
Boating on the Pegnitz River	87
Chapter 8	**89**
Food & Drinks – A Culinary Journey	89
Must-Try Local Dishes (Bratwurst, Lebkuchen & More)	90
Fine Dining & Michelin-Starred Restaurants	93
Best Traditional Bavarian Beer Gardens	95

Street Food & Casual Dining Spots	97
Vegetarian & Vegan Options in Nuremberg	98
Chapter 9	**102**
Nuremberg's Nightlife & Entertainment	102
Best Bars & Pubs for a Great Night Out	103
Live Music Venues & Concert Halls	105
Theater & Cultural Performances	107
Unique Nighttime Experiences in Nuremberg	108
Chapter 10	**111**
Shopping in Nuremberg	111
Where to Buy Authentic Nuremberg Souvenirs	111
Best Shopping Streets & Markets	113
Luxury Boutiques & Local Artisan Shops	116
Christmas Markets: A Winter Wonderland	117
Chapter 11	**126**
7 Must-Do Things in Nuremberg	126
Chapter 12	**135**
Day Trips & Excursions from Nuremberg	135
Bamberg: The Little Venice Of Bavaria	136
Rothenburg Ob Der Tauber: A Fairytale Town	138
Regensburg: A Unesco Heritage Gem	139
Franconian Wine Country: A Hidden Treasure	141
Dachau Concentration Camp Memorial Site	142
Chapter 13	**145**

Nuremberg for Different Types of Travelers	145
Solo Travelers: Safety & Must-Know Tips	145
Romantic Getaways for Couples	147
Family-Friendly Activities & Attractions in Nuremberg	149
Budget Travel: Saving Money While Enjoying Nuremberg	156
Luxury Travel: Exclusive Experiences	160
Chapter 14	**165**
Suggested Itineraries for Every Traveler	165
One-Day Express Tour of Nuremberg	165
A 3-Day Nuremberg Itinerary	168
5-Day Itinerary with Excursions	170
The Ultimate Week-Long Adventure	174
Chapter 15	**177**
Hidden Gems & Insider Tips in Nuremberg	177
Secret Spots Only Locals Know	178
Underrated Parks & Gardens for a Tranquil Escape	181
Where to Find the Best Views of Nuremberg	183
Unusual Experiences & Off-the-Beaten-Path Adventures	184
Chapter 16	**187**
Sustainable & Responsible Travel in Nuremberg	187
Eco-Friendly Hotels and Stays – Where to Stay Sustainably	188
Supporting Local Businesses – How to Travel Ethically	190
Public Transport & Bike Rentals – Green Ways to Get Around	191

Nuremberg's Green Initiatives – How the City Stays Sustainable
                                                                    193

Chapter 17   **195**

Practical Information for a Stress-Free Trip   195

Safety and Health Tips & Emergency Contacts   196

Currency Exchange & Payment Methods   199

Useful German Phrases for Travelers   201

SIM Cards & Wi-Fi Access in Nuremberg   206

Best Apps for Navigating the City   208

Conclusion   **212**

Channah David

Channah David

Welcome to Nuremberg

Some cities capture the eye, and then some seize the soul—Nuremberg belongs to the latter. This Bavarian gem is not just a place on a map but a journey through time, a story written in cobblestone streets and whispered by ancient towers. If you think you know Germany, prepare to be surprised. Nuremberg is where medieval collides with modern creativity, where history is not confined to museums but unfolds before you in every square, every alley, and every half-timbered house.

Stepping into Nuremberg is like turning the pages of a living history book, each chapter more intriguing than the last. This is the city that once set the stage for emperors, artists, and revolutionaries. It's a place where Gothic churches loom with an almost otherworldly presence, where castle walls still hold the echoes of bygone battles, and where traditional Christmas markets turn the streets into a twinkling fairytale wonderland. But beyond its historical weight, Nuremberg is fiercely alive—a city that pulsates with innovation, from its cutting-edge museums and thriving arts scene to its vibrant beer gardens and culinary delights.

Yet, Nuremberg isn't just about grand monuments or postcard-perfect streets; it's about the details—the scent of fresh gingerbread wafting through the air, the murmur of the Pegnitz River as you cross the Fleisch Bridge, the way the golden light of sunset bathes the Hauptmarkt in a glow that makes time feel irrelevant. It's about the stories hidden in underground tunnels, the craftsmanship of artisans in tucked-away workshops, and the feeling of being enveloped in a city that is both timeless and ever-evolving.

This guide is your key to unlocking the true essence of Nuremberg. Whether you're here to trace the city's medieval past, indulge in Franconian specialties, or uncover its modern pulse, every page is designed to take you deeper into its wonders. Forget the surface-level travel advice—this book goes beyond the expected, bringing you expert insights, hidden gems, and the kind of insider knowledge that transforms a trip into an unforgettable adventure.

So, welcome to Nuremberg—where every moment is a masterpiece, every street tells a story, and every traveler becomes part of its legend.

Why Nuremberg in 2025?

There has never been a better time to visit Nuremberg than in 2025. The city continues to evolve, offering a unique mix of tradition and modernity that captivates visitors from around the globe. Here's why Nuremberg should be on your travel radar this year:

1. A City Steeped in History

Nuremberg's historical significance is unparalleled. The city played a pivotal role in the Holy Roman Empire, the Renaissance period, and even World War II, making it a place of profound cultural and historical importance. In 2025, new museum exhibitions, immersive historical tours, and restored heritage sites will offer deeper insights into its rich past.

2. A Thriving Cultural Scene

The city is an artistic hub, hosting world-class museums, music festivals, and theatrical performances. The Albrecht Dürer House, Germanisches National Museum, and Dokumentationszentrum continue to offer fresh exhibits and insights, making 2025 a great year for culture lovers.

3. World-Class Events & Festivals

Nuremberg's event calendar is packed with exciting happenings in 2025. From the renowned Christkindlesmarkt in December to the International Toy Fair and Rock im Park music festival, there's always something happening. Plus, the city will be hosting new art and technology festivals that celebrate its innovative spirit.

4. Culinary Renaissance

Nuremberg's food scene is undergoing a renaissance, blending traditional Bavarian flavors with modern gourmet experiences. From authentic Nuremberg bratwurst and Lebkuchen to Michelin-starred restaurants and craft beer havens, 2025 promises a fantastic culinary journey.

5. A Sustainable Travel Destination

Nuremberg has taken significant steps towards sustainability, making it a greener city to visit. With an extensive public transportation network, bike-friendly streets, and eco-conscious hotels and restaurants, it's easier than ever to travel responsibly while exploring its many wonders.

6. Convenient Access & Connectivity

With excellent train connections, a well-connected international airport, and an efficient public transit system, getting to and around Nuremberg has never been easier. In 2025, expect even more seamless travel options, including expanded high-speed rail links and smart city navigation tools.

7. Perfect for Every Traveler

Whether you're a solo adventurer, a couple seeking romance, a family on vacation, or a luxury traveler looking for indulgent experiences, Nuremberg caters to all types of visitors. From charming boutique hotels to world-class resorts, there's a perfect place for every traveler to stay and explore.

Chapter 1

Travel Planning & Essentials

Planning a trip to Nuremberg, Germany, requires thoughtful preparation to ensure a seamless and enriching experience. This chapter delves into the crucial aspects of travel planning, including entry requirements, optimal visiting periods, cultural nuances, and packing essentials tailored to each season.

Entry Requirements: Visas, COVID-19 Guidelines & Travel Insurance

Before embarking on your journey to Nuremberg, it's imperative to understand the entry protocols to avoid any unforeseen complications.

Visas

Germany is a member of the Schengen Area, allowing for streamlined travel across many European countries. Depending on your nationality, visa requirements may vary:

- **EU/EEA Citizens**: Travelers from the European Union or European Economic Area countries can enter Germany without a visa, using a valid passport or national ID card.

- **Non-EU/EEA Citizens**: Visitors from countries like the United States, Canada, Australia, and several others can enter Germany visa-free for short stays (up to 90 days within 180 days) for tourism or business purposes.

However, starting in 2025, the European Union will implement the European Travel Information and Authorization System (ETIAS), requiring travelers from visa-exempt countries to obtain an online authorization before arrival.

- **Other Nationalities**: If your country isn't on the visa-exempt list, you'll need to apply for a Schengen visa at the German consulate or embassy in your home country. It's advisable to initiate this process well in advance of your planned departure.

COVID-19 Guidelines

As of March 2025, Germany has adapted its COVID-19 protocols in line with global health developments. While many restrictions have been lifted, it's essential to stay informed:

- **Vaccination**: Travelers are encouraged to be fully vaccinated with vaccines recognized by the European Medicines Agency (EMA). Carry proof of vaccination, as some establishments may still require it.

- **Testing**: Although routine testing mandates have been relaxed, unvaccinated travelers might need to present a negative PCR or antigen test taken within 48 hours before arrival.

- **Health Declarations**: Some regions may require health declaration forms or digital check-ins. It's prudent to check the latest requirements before your trip.

Travel Insurance

While not mandatory, comprehensive travel insurance is highly recommended. A good policy should cover:

- **Medical Emergencies**: Including COVID-19 related treatments.

- **Trip Cancellations or Interruptions**: To safeguard against unforeseen events.

- **Lost or Delayed Baggage**: Ensuring you're covered for any inconveniences.

Best Time to Visit: Seasons, Weather & Festivals

Nuremberg offers distinct experiences throughout the year, each season bringing its unique charm.

Spring (March to May)

- **Weather**: Temperatures range from 5°C to 15°C, with blooming flowers and rejuvenated greenery.

- **Festivals**: The Nuremberg Spring Festival, akin to a mini-Oktoberfest, features traditional Bavarian music, food, and rides.

Summer (June to August)

- **Weather**: Warm and pleasant, averaging between 15°C to 25°C.

- **Festivals**: The Bardentreffen Festival, one of Germany's largest world music festivals, takes place in late July, attracting artists and visitors worldwide.

Autumn (September to November)

- **Weather**: Cooler temperatures between 10°C and 20°C, with picturesque fall foliage.

- **Festivals**: The Nuremberg Old Town Festival in September celebrates Franconian culture with traditional music, dance, and culinary delights.

Winter (December to February)

- **Weather**: Cold, with temperatures ranging from -2°C to 5°C. Snowfall adds a magical touch to the cityscape.

- **Festivals**: The world-renowned Nuremberg Christkindlesmarkt, one of the oldest Christmas markets, transforms the city into a winter wonderland from late November to December 24th.

Language & Cultural Etiquette

Understanding local customs enhances your travel experience and fosters respectful interactions.

Language

- **German** is the official language. While many locals speak English, especially in tourist areas, learning basic German phrases can enrich your interactions.

Cultural Etiquette

- **Greetings**: A firm handshake with direct eye contact is customary. Address individuals using "Herr" (Mr.) or "Frau" (Ms.) followed by their surname until invited to use their first name.
- **Punctuality**: Germans value timeliness. Arriving late can be perceived as disrespectful.
- **Dining**: Wait to be seated in restaurants. When toasting, maintain eye contact and say "Prost!" Tipping around 5-10% is customary, given directly to the server.
- **Dress Code**: Casual attire is acceptable, but opt for smart-casual when dining out or attending events.

Packing List: What to Bring for Every Season

Packing appropriately ensures comfort and preparedness for Nuremberg's varying climates.

Spring

- **Clothing**: Light layers, including long-sleeve shirts, lightweight sweaters, and a medium-weight jacket.

- **Footwear**: Comfortable walking shoes suitable for city exploration.

- **Accessories**: An umbrella or raincoat, as spring showers are common.

Summer

- **Clothing**: Breathable fabrics like cotton or linen, shorts, and t-shirts.

- **Footwear**: Sandals or lightweight sneakers.

- **Accessories**: Sunglasses, a hat, and sunscreen to protect against the sun.

Autumn

- **Clothing**: Layers such as sweaters, long pants, and a warm jacket.

- **Footwear**: Waterproof shoes or boots, considering potential rain.

- **Accessories**: A scarf and gloves for cooler evenings.

Winter

- **Clothing**: Thermal layers, heavy coats, sweaters, and insulated pants.
- **Footwear**: Waterproof, insulated boots with good traction for snowy conditions.
- **Accessories**: Hats, gloves, scarves, and thermal socks.

Insider Tip

For an authentic Nuremberg experience, time your visit during the Christkindlesmarkt. Beyond the festive stalls, explore the lesser-known "Feuerzangenbowle" gatherings—a traditional German mulled wine punch set aflame, offering warmth and cheer amidst the winter chill.

By meticulously planning your trip with these essentials in mind, you're set to immerse yourself fully in the rich history, culture, and festivities that Nuremberg graciously offers.

Chapter 2

Getting to Nuremberg

Nuremberg, a city steeped in medieval charm and modern convenience, is a well-connected travel hub that seamlessly welcomes visitors. Whether you're arriving by air, train, or car, or navigating the city's efficient public transportation network, knowing the best ways to get here and move around ensures a hassle-free trip. This chapter provides an in-depth guide on reaching Nuremberg and exploring it with ease.

Arriving by Air: Nuremberg Airport Guide

For international and domestic travelers, Nuremberg Airport (Albrecht Dürer Airport, NUE) is the city's primary air gateway. Conveniently located just 5 km (3 miles) north of the city center, the airport is well-equipped with modern facilities and efficient transport links.

Airlines & Destinations

- **Domestic Flights**: Lufthansa and Eurowings provide frequent connections to Frankfurt, Munich, and Berlin.

- **European Destinations**: Direct flights to major hubs like London, Paris, Amsterdam, Vienna, and Madrid.

- **International Travel**: While long-haul flights are limited, Frankfurt and Munich airports serve as key transfer points.

Airport Facilities & Services

- **Transport Connections**: The U2 subway line runs directly from the airport to the city center in under 15 minutes.

- **Car Rentals**: Major providers like Sixt, Europcar, and Hertz have counters at the airport.

- **Lounge & Dining**: The Airport Lounge offers premium services, while eateries like Marché Mövenpick serve regional specialties.

Navigating the Airport

- **Security & Immigration**: Typically efficient, with wait times averaging 10-15 minutes.

- **Currency Exchange & ATMs**: Multiple banks and currency exchange booths are available.

- **Luggage Services**: Lockers and baggage wrapping are accessible in the arrivals hall.

Traveling by Train: Nuremberg's Rail Connections

Nuremberg's Hauptbahnhof (Central Station) is one of Germany's busiest railway hubs, offering seamless connections to cities across Europe.

High-Speed Rail (ICE, IC & EC Services)

- **Frankfurt to Nuremberg**: 2 hours via ICE high-speed trains.

- **Munich to Nuremberg**: Just over an hour, making it a perfect day-trip option.

- **Berlin to Nuremberg**: Around 3 hours, thanks to Deutsche Bahn's efficient ICE services.

- **Vienna to Nuremberg**: Approximately 4 hours via direct trains.

Regional & International Trains

- **S-Bahn & RE Trains**: Connect smaller Bavarian towns like Bamberg, Regensburg, and Würzburg.

- **Cross-Border Travel**: Direct trains to Prague (Czech Republic) and Innsbruck (Austria) provide scenic international routes.

Station Amenities

- **Shops & Dining**: The station houses a variety of bakeries, cafés, and convenience stores.

- **Luggage Lockers**: Available in different sizes for short-term storage.

- **Public Transport Access**: The Hauptbahnhof integrates with the tram, bus, and U-Bahn network.

Road Trip to Nuremberg: Driving & Parking Tips

Driving to Nuremberg can be a scenic and flexible way to explore Bavaria, but knowing road rules and parking options is essential.

Driving Routes & Highways

- **From Munich**: Via the A9 Autobahn, approximately 170 km (105 miles), a 1.5-hour drive.

- **From Frankfurt**: Via the A3 Autobahn, covering 225 km (140 miles) in about 2.5 hours.
- **From Prague**: A 3.5-hour drive via the A6 Autobahn, passing through picturesque countryside.

Parking in Nuremberg

- **City Center Parking**: Underground garages such as Parkhaus Adlerstraße and Parkhaus Hauptmarkt are convenient but often fill up quickly.
- **Park & Ride (P+R) Lots**: Budget-friendly options outside the city, with tram connections to the center.
- **Street Parking**: Limited and metered, with time restrictions in many areas.

Driving Tips

- **Low Emission Zones**: Nuremberg enforces environmental regulations requiring a green emissions sticker for vehicles entering the city.

- **Speed Limits**: Autobahns may have unrestricted speed sections, but urban areas are strictly limited to 50 km/h (31 mph).

- **Toll Roads**: While Germany doesn't have general tolls for private vehicles, certain tunnels and bridges may have fees.

Public Transport Overview: Trams, Buses & Bike Rentals

Nuremberg boasts an efficient and tourist-friendly public transport system, making car-free exploration seamless.

U-Bahn (Subway) System

- **Key Lines**: The U1, U2, and U3 lines cover major tourist areas, including the Hauptbahnhof, Altstadt (Old Town), and Messe (Exhibition Center).

- **Tickets & Passes**:
    - Single ride: €3.20

- Day pass: €8.20
- Nürnberg Card: Provides free transport and museum entry.

Tram Network

- **Best Routes for Visitors**:
  - **Tram 4**: Connects the central station to the historic district.
  - **Tram 6**: A scenic route passing by cultural landmarks.
- **Frequency**: Trams run every 10-15 minutes, with late-night services on weekends.

Bus Services

- **Night Buses**: Operate after midnight, ensuring safe travel for night owls.
- **Airport Bus**: Line 30 connects the airport with key areas beyond the U-Bahn route.

Bike Rentals & E-Scooters

- **Bike-Sharing**: Services like VAG Rad allow affordable bike rentals throughout the city.

- **E-Scooters**: Lime and Tier operate scooter rentals, ideal for short-distance travel.

- **Cycling Paths**: Nuremberg has dedicated lanes, making biking a safe and enjoyable option.

Insider Tip

For a seamless arrival experience, take the U2 subway from the airport to the city center—it's faster, cheaper, and more convenient than taxis. If traveling by train, grab a fresh pretzel from one of the Hauptbahnhof's legendary bakeries to start your Nuremberg journey the Bavarian way!

Chapter 3

Where to Stay in Nuremberg

Welcome to Nuremberg, a city where medieval charm meets modern elegance. Selecting the perfect accommodation is pivotal to enhancing your travel experience. In this chapter, we'll explore a spectrum of lodging options, from opulent luxury hotels to cozy budget-friendly stays, ensuring your visit is both comfortable and memorable.

Luxury Hotels – Iconic 5-Star Accommodations

For travelers seeking unparalleled elegance and top-tier amenities, Nuremberg offers a selection of luxury hotels that blend historical grandeur with contemporary sophistication.

Sheraton Carlton Hotel Nürnberg

Situated near the historic Old Town, the Sheraton Carlton Hotel Nürnberg provides guests with spacious rooms, an exquisite spa, and a rooftop terrace offering panoramic city views. Its proximity to major attractions makes it a favored choice for those wishing to explore the city in style.

Le Méridien Grand Hotel Nürnberg

Facing the main railway station, Le Méridien Grand Hotel Nürnberg is a testament to timeless luxury. With its classic architecture and modern amenities, guests can enjoy gourmet dining and elegantly furnished rooms, all within walking distance of Nuremberg's cultural landmarks.

Sheraton Carlton Hotel

Mid-Range Comfort – Best Value-for-Money Hotels

Travelers desiring comfort without the extravagant price tag will find Nuremberg's mid-range hotels to be both accommodating and reasonably priced.

Novina Hotel Wöhrdersee

Adina Apartment Hotel Nuremberg

Located adjacent to the Germanic National Museum, the Adina Apartment Hotel offers spacious apartments equipped with full kitchens. Guests can also enjoy an indoor swimming pool and fitness center, making it ideal for both short and extended stays.

Novina Hotel Wöhrdersee Nürnberg City

Nestled near Wöhrder Lake, this hotel combines natural beauty with urban convenience. A short walk from the main train station, it offers modern rooms and easy access to scenic jogging and cycling paths around the lake.

Budget-Friendly Stays – Hostels and Affordable Lodging

For the budget-conscious traveler, Nuremberg provides several options that ensure a pleasant stay without straining the wallet.

Five Reasons Hotel & Hostel

Located in the heart of the city, Five Reasons offers both private rooms and dormitories. With a communal kitchen and lounge area, it's perfect for travelers seeking affordability without compromising on location or comfort.

Hostel Nürnberg

This centrally located hostel provides clean and simple accommodations, making it a favorite among backpackers and solo travelers. Its proximity to public transportation and major sights adds to its appeal.

Unique Stays – Boutique Hotels and Historic Inns

Five Reasons Hotel & Hostel

For those yearning for a distinctive lodging experience, Nuremberg's boutique hotels and historic inns offer charm and personalized service.

Hotel Drei Raben

Each room in Hotel Drei Raben is uniquely themed, narrating tales from Nuremberg's rich history and legends. This boutique hotel's intimate atmosphere and attention to detail provide a truly memorable stay.

Hotel Elch

Set in a 14th-century timber-framed building, Hotel Elch seamlessly blends historic ambiance with modern comforts. Its location in the Old Town's serene lanes offers guests a peaceful retreat amidst the city's vibrant culture.

Best Areas to Stay: Old Town vs. Outer Districts

Choosing the right neighborhood can significantly influence your Nuremberg experience. Here's a comparison to guide your decision:

Old Town (Altstadt)

Pros:

- **Historical Significance:** Staying in the Old Town immerses you in Nuremberg's rich past, with landmarks like the Imperial Castle and St. Lorenz Church just steps away.

- **Convenience:** A plethora of restaurants, shops, and cultural sites are within walking distance, reducing the need for extensive travel.

Cons:

- **Cost:** Accommodations here can be pricier due to the central location and high demand.

- **Noise Levels:** The bustling tourist activity might result in higher noise levels, which could be a consideration for light sleepers.

Outer Districts

Pros:

- **Tranquility:** Areas like Marienvorstadt offer a peaceful environment, often with more green spaces and less hustle and bustle.

- **Affordability:** Accommodations tend to be more budget-friendly, providing excellent value for money.

Cons:

- **Distance:** While public transport is efficient, staying outside the city center means longer travel times to major attractions.

- **Limited Nightlife:** The outer districts may have fewer dining and entertainment options compared to the vibrant Old Town.

Insider Tip: If you're visiting during major events like the Nuremberg Christmas Market, booking accommodations well in advance is advisable, as the city attracts numerous visitors, leading to limited availability and higher prices.

Map Showing various Hotels in Nuremberg

Chapter 4

Exploring Nuremberg's Old Town (Altstadt)

The Old Town (Altstadt) of Nuremberg is a captivating fusion of medieval beauty, historic grandeur, and contemporary energy. The Altstadt, which is surrounded by well-preserved city walls, provides tourists with a trip back in time. Cobblestone streets lead to breathtaking architectural marvels, bustling marketplaces, and cultural treasures. This chapter explores the most famous sites, exposing their fascinating pasts and essential information for a trip that will never be forgotten.

Hauptmarkt – The Heart of the City

The Hauptmarkt is the bustling central square of Nuremberg, known for its vibrant atmosphere, historical significance, and the world-famous Nuremberg Christmas Market.

A Marketplace with Centuries of History

Dating back to the Middle Ages, the Hauptmarkt has been the beating heart of commerce in Nuremberg. Today, it remains a lively center for locals and tourists alike, offering fresh produce, handcrafted goods, and regional delicacies.

The Nuremberg Christmas Market (Christkindlesmarkt)

Christkindlesmarkt

Held annually during the advent season, this market is one of the most famous in Germany. Thousands of glowing stalls offer traditional wooden ornaments, spiced gingerbread (Lebkuchen), and steaming cups of mulled wine (Glühwein). The market's opening ceremony is led by the Christkind, a symbolic angelic figure central to Nuremberg's Christmas tradition.

Frauenkirche – A Gothic Masterpiece Overlooking Hauptmarkt

On the eastern side of the square stands the Frauenkirche, a stunning 14th-century Gothic church. Every day at noon, visitors gather to witness the mechanical procession of figures known as the Männleinlaufen, commemorating Emperor Charles IV's Golden Bull of 1356.

Insider Tip

If you're visiting outside the Christmas season, the Hauptmarkt still hosts an array of seasonal markets, including the Easter Market and local farmers' markets, making it a lively destination year-round.

Nuremberg Castle (Kaiserburg) – A Step Back in Time

Perched atop a sandstone hill, Nuremberg Castle dominates the city skyline, serving as a symbol of the city's medieval power and imperial significance.

The Imperial Residence of the Holy Roman Emperors

From the 11th century onwards, the Kaiserburg was an important seat of the Holy Roman Empire. The castle was not only a military fortress but also a residence for emperors, shaping the political and cultural history of Nuremberg.

Must-See Highlights Within the Castle

Nuremberg Castle

- **Sinwell Tower:** This towering structure offers panoramic views of the Old Town, making it a perfect spot for breathtaking photos.

- **Deep Well (Tiefe Brunnen):** A marvel of medieval engineering, this well plunges 50 meters into the rock, demonstrating how the fortress secured water supply during sieges.

- **Imperial Chapel:** A remarkable Romanesque-style chapel that showcases the religious significance of the castle.

Exploring the Castle Grounds

The castle complex includes beautifully restored courtyards, medieval defense walls, and a fascinating museum exhibiting artifacts from Nuremberg's imperial past.

Insider Tip

Arrive early in the morning or late in the afternoon to avoid crowds and fully appreciate the grandeur of the castle in peaceful solitude.

Schöner Brunnen – The Beautiful Fountain and Its Legend

Located at the edge of the Hauptmarkt, the Schöner Brunnen is a masterpiece of medieval craftsmanship, steeped in symbolism and legend.

A Jewel of Gothic Architecture

Erected in the 14th century, this 19-meter-high fountain is adorned with 40 exquisitely carved figures representing philosophers, church leaders, electors, and Holy Roman Emperors. The vibrant gold, red, and blue accents make it one of the most eye-catching landmarks in the Altstadt.

Schöner Brunnen

The Golden Ring Myth

A unique feature of the fountain is its rotating brass ring embedded within the wrought iron fence. According to local legend, turning the ring three times brings good luck and ensures a return to Nuremberg. Whether or not the myth holds, spinning the ring remains a cherished tradition among visitors.

Insider Tip: Look closely at the ironwork—there's a second, hidden black ring. Legend says spinning this one grants even greater fortune, though fewer tourists know about it!

St. Sebald and St. Lorenz Churches – Gothic Marvels

Nuremberg's skyline is defined by the towering spires of St. Sebald and St. Lorenz, two magnificent Gothic churches that have stood the test of time, surviving wars and centuries of transformation. These churches are not just places of worship but also architectural masterpieces adorned with priceless art and historical significance.

St. Sebald – Nuremberg's Patron Saint and His Church

Built in the 13th century, St. Sebald Church is dedicated to Nuremberg's patron saint. Its twin towers rise above the city, guiding visitors toward a sanctuary filled with religious relics, intricate sculptures, and breathtaking stained glass.

- **The Shrine of St. Sebald:** This silver-and-bronze masterpiece houses the relics of the city's patron saint, designed by the renowned Peter Vischer the Elder.

- **Medieval Murals and Altars:** Inside, visitors will find well-preserved frescoes and altars that tell the biblical story through Gothic artistry.

- **Organ Recitals:** St. Sebald is famous for its majestic organ concerts, where the deep resonance of centuries-old pipes fills the ancient stone nave.

St. Lorenz – A Testament to Nuremberg's Artistic Brilliance

A short walk away, St. Lorenz Church boasts an equally breathtaking design. Its soaring Gothic façade is adorned with sculptures, while inside, visitors are greeted by immense vaults and elaborate religious artwork.

- **The Angelic Salutation:** One of the most famous sculptures in the church, created by Veit Stoss, this intricate wooden carving of the

Annunciation is suspended from the ceiling and radiates divine beauty.

- **The Stained Glass Windows:** Dating back to the Middle Ages, the massive stained glass windows flood the church with ethereal light, depicting biblical scenes in rich colors.

- **The Tower Views:** Climbing St. Lorenz's towers rewards visitors with one of the best panoramic views of Nuremberg.

Insider Tip

If you're lucky, you might hear the church bells ringing in unison, an awe-inspiring sound that echoes through the Old Town, creating a truly medieval atmosphere.

Albrecht Dürer's House – The Home of a Renaissance Master

Few artists have left as indelible a mark on Nuremberg as Albrecht Dürer, the Renaissance painter, printmaker, and theorist. His former residence, now a museum, provides an intimate glimpse into the daily life and creative genius of one of Germany's greatest artists.

A Glimpse into a Genius's Life

Dürer lived in this half-timbered house from 1509 until he died in 1528. Today, visitors can walk through the same halls where he created his masterpieces, gaining insight into the life of a Renaissance artist.

Albrecht Dürer's House

- **The Recreated Workshop:** The museum features a reconstructed studio where Dürer produced his famous engravings, such as *Melencolia I* and *The Rhinoceros*.

- **Historical Living Quarters:** Explore the 16th-century kitchen, bedroom, and workspaces furnished with period-accurate details.

- **Original and Reproduction Works:** While most original Dürer pieces are housed in major art museums worldwide, this museum displays high-quality reproductions and detailed descriptions of his artistic techniques.

The Courtyard and the Dürer Rabbit

Outside the house, a bronze sculpture of a giant hare pays tribute to one of Dürer's most famous sketches, *Young Hare*. The courtyard itself is a charming spot to take in the medieval atmosphere.

Insider Tip: Visit during a guided demonstration of Dürer's printmaking techniques to see how his intricate engravings were created by hand.

Weißgerbergasse – The Most Picturesque Street

Tucked away in the heart of the Old Town, Weißgerbergasse is one of Nuremberg's most picturesque and well-preserved medieval streets. Its name, which translates to "Tanners' Alley," reflects its history as a center for leatherworking during the Middle Ages.

A Step Back in Time

Strolling down Weißgerbergasse is like stepping into a fairy tale. The street is lined with over 20 traditional half-timbered houses, many dating back to the 16th century. Their colorful facades, adorned with wooden beams and flower boxes, create a postcard-perfect scene.

- **Medieval Craftsmanship:** Many of the houses retain their original architectural features, including beautifully carved doorways and wooden shutters.

- **Boutique Shops and Cafés:** Today, the street is home to charming local boutiques, artisan workshops, and cozy cafés, making it an ideal spot to pause and enjoy the ambiance.

- **Photography Hotspot:** The play of light on the cobblestones and the vibrant hues of the buildings make this street a favorite for photographers and Instagram enthusiasts.

A Living Legacy

Unlike many medieval streets in Europe that have been overly commercialized, Weißgerbergasse has managed to retain its authenticity. Many of the buildings remain privately owned residences, preserving the quiet, intimate atmosphere of this hidden gem.

Insider Tip

For a truly magical experience, visit in the early morning or at dusk when the street is bathed in golden light, and you can enjoy its beauty without the crowds.

With its towering Gothic churches, the artistic legacy of Albrecht Dürer, and the timeless charm of Weißgerbergasse, this chapter has explored some of Nuremberg's most captivating treasures. These landmarks offer a deep dive into the city's artistic and architectural history, each telling a unique story of Nuremberg's past and its enduring cultural significance.

Chapter 5

Top Attractions in Nuremberg

In the city of Nuremberg, modernity, culture, and history all coexist harmoniously. Nuremberg offers something for everyone, whether you are interested in history, or art, or just want to experience the ambiance of a medieval city with a thriving modern culture. To give you the most immersive experience possible, this chapter walks you through the must-see sights that characterize this famous Bavarian city.

Kaiserburg Nuremberg – The Imperial Castle

Standing proudly above the city, the **Kaiserburg (Imperial Castle)** is Nuremberg's most iconic landmark. This medieval fortress was once the residence of the Holy Roman Emperors and remains a symbol of the city's importance during the Middle Ages.

Highlights of the Castle:

- **Sinwell Tower** – Climb to the top for breathtaking panoramic views of the city.

- **The Deep Well** – A fascinating structure that plunges 50 meters into the rock, demonstrating medieval engineering.

- **The Double Chapel** – A stunning architectural masterpiece that showcases Romanesque and Gothic styles.

The castle's museum provides in-depth historical insights, showcasing medieval weapons, armor, and artifacts. Walking through its stone corridors transports you back to an era of knights and emperors.

The Hauptmarkt and Schöner Brunnen

The **Hauptmarkt** is the beating heart of Nuremberg's Old Town. This bustling square is home to one of Germany's most famous Christmas markets, but it remains lively throughout the year.

Key Attractions at the Hauptmarkt:

- **Schöner Brunnen (Beautiful Fountain)** – A 14th-century fountain adorned with intricate figures representing the Holy Roman Empire.

- **The Market Stalls** – Offering everything from fresh produce to Bavarian delicacies like Lebkuchen (gingerbread).

- **Frauenkirche (Church of Our Lady)** – A stunning Gothic church with an astronomical clock that performs daily at noon.

Visiting the Hauptmarkt is an essential Nuremberg experience, offering a glimpse into the city's lively culture and deep-rooted traditions.

Documentation Center Nazi Party Rally Grounds

For those seeking a deeper understanding of Nuremberg's role in world history, the **Documentation Center at the Nazi Party Rally Grounds** is a sobering yet essential stop.

What to Expect:

- **Permanent Exhibition: 'Fascination and Terror'** – A detailed look into the rise and impact of the Nazi regime.

- **The Grandstand (Zeppelintribüne)** – One of the few remaining structures from the Nazi rally grounds, offering a chilling look at history.

- **Educational Tours and Multimedia Displays** – Providing context to one of the darkest chapters in human history.

Documentation Center at the Nazi Party Rally Grounds

This museum is a must-visit for anyone interested in understanding the profound effects of the 20th century on Nuremberg and beyond.

Germanisches Nationalmuseum – A Journey Through Time

Housing one of the most comprehensive collections of German art and culture, the **Germanisches Nationalmuseum** is a treasure trove for history and art lovers.

Museum Highlights:

- **Medieval and Renaissance Art** – Featuring paintings, sculptures, and artifacts from Germany's rich artistic past.

- **The Oldest Surviving Globe** – The famous Behaim Globe from the 15th century.

- **Contemporary and Modern Exhibits** – Showcasing innovations in German design and craftsmanship.

A visit to this museum is a deep dive into Germany's cultural heritage, spanning from ancient times to the modern era.

Nuremberg Zoo – A Natural Escape

For families and wildlife enthusiasts, the **Nuremberg Zoo** offers an incredible experience amidst lush greenery. One of Germany's largest zoological gardens, this zoo is home to over 300 species.

Must-See Attractions in the Zoo:

- **Dolphin Lagoon** – One of the only places in Europe where you can see dolphins in a semi-natural environment.

- **The Manatee House** – A fascinating exhibit dedicated to these gentle aquatic mammals.

- **Polar Bear Habitat** – Home to majestic polar bears in a setting that mimics their natural Arctic environment.

The zoo's beautifully landscaped grounds make it a peaceful retreat from the city's bustling streets.

Albrecht Dürer's House – A Glimpse into a Genius's Life

One of Nuremberg's most famous sons, **Albrecht Dürer**, was a Renaissance master whose influence on art is undeniable. His **half-timbered house**, preserved as a museum, provides insight into his life and work.

What You'll Find Inside:

- **Dürer's Studio** – A recreated artist's workshop showcasing his tools and techniques.

- **Original Prints and Replicas** – See some of his most famous works up close.

- **Historical Exhibits on Renaissance Life** – A deeper look into the era in which Dürer lived and worked.

This attraction is a must-visit for art lovers and those interested in Nuremberg's rich cultural history.

Insider Tip

For the best experience at the Hauptmarkt, visit early in the morning to enjoy the square without the crowds. If you're in Nuremberg during Christmas, the Christkindlesmarkt is an unmissable event filled with festive stalls, twinkling lights, and traditional treats.

Map Showing various Top Attractions in Nuremberg

Chapter 6

Nuremberg's Must-Visit Museums

History permeates Nuremberg's streets, medieval splendor coexists with the important lessons learned from the past, and museums act as entry points to a greater understanding of the city. Whether you are a history buff, art enthusiast, or just a curious tourist, Nuremberg's museums provide a rich and varied experience. This chapter examines the must-see establishments that illuminate Nuremberg's rich and complicated past, from the biggest cultural museum in Germany to the eerily important Nazi Documentation Center.

Germanisches Nationalmuseum – The Largest Cultural Museum In Germany

Stepping into the **Germanisches Nationalmuseum (GNM)** is like walking through a time portal that stretches back over a thousand years. Established in 1852, this massive institution houses over **1.3 million artifacts**, making it Germany's most extensive museum dedicated to cultural history. Located near the historic city walls, this museum is not just a collection of objects but a narrative of German-speaking Europe's artistic and intellectual heritage.

Germanisches Nationalmuseum

What You'll Discover Inside:

- **Medieval Masterpieces:** The museum holds an awe-inspiring collection of medieval armor, sculptures, and paintings. The **Epiphany Altar by Hans Baldung Grien** and works by **Albrecht Dürer** are particularly captivating.

- **The Oldest Globe in the World:** The famous **Erdapfel (Earth Apple)**, crafted in 1492, is believed to be the oldest surviving terrestrial globe, providing a glimpse into how early explorers perceived the world.

- **Scientific and Musical Instruments:** From ancient astrolabes to early keyboard instruments, this section highlights Germany's contributions to science and music.

- **18th and 19th Century Art & Fashion:** Elegant garments from the Baroque period, beautifully preserved, showcase the evolution of style and craftsmanship.

- **The Hall of Historical Arms:** Featuring a vast array of swords, armor, and firearms, this section delves into the martial history of the German-speaking world.

Why It's a Must-Visit:

The museum is **not just about history; it's about storytelling.** Each artifact connects to a broader narrative about European culture, identity, and artistic evolution. With meticulously curated exhibits and an extensive collection, **the GNM is an unmissable experience for anyone looking to dive deep into the essence of German heritage.**

Insider Tip

The museum can be overwhelming due to its size. Consider taking a **guided tour** to focus on key exhibits, and don't miss the museum's tranquil inner courtyard—a hidden gem ideal for a peaceful break.

Documentation Center Nazi Party Rally Grounds – Understanding History

Few places in the world encapsulate the weight of history as powerfully as the **Dokumentationszentrum**

Reichsparteitagsgelände (Documentation Center Nazi Party Rally Grounds). Located on the site of Hitler's massive, unfinished **Congress Hall**, this museum offers a profound, unflinching look at how propaganda fueled one of history's darkest chapters.

Exploring the Museum:

- **Permanent Exhibition: "Fascination and Terror"** – This harrowing yet essential exhibit examines the rise of National Socialism, the events leading to WWII, and the consequences of dictatorship.

- **The Unfinished Congress Hall:** Initially designed to hold 50,000 people, this structure stands as an eerie monument to Nazi ambitions. Its sheer size reflects the regime's obsession with power and control.

- **First-Hand Accounts:** Letters, speeches, and video testimonies from victims, survivors, and former Nazi members provide a deeply personal connection to history.

- **Interactive Multimedia Displays:** Touchscreens and digital archives allow visitors to delve into wartime records and explore propaganda's psychological effects.

- **The Rally Grounds Tour:** Beyond the museum, visitors can explore the remnants of the Zeppelin Field and Luitpold Arena, once used for massive Nazi rallies. Walking through these locations is a haunting, reflective experience.

Why It's a Must-Visit: Understanding history is crucial to ensuring that its darkest moments are never repeated. This museum is not about glorifying the past but about confronting it head-on, educating visitors on the dangers of totalitarianism and the mechanisms of propaganda.

Insider Tip

The emotional weight of the exhibits can be overwhelming. If you need a break, take a walk around **Dutzendteich Lake**, just outside the museum, to reflect and decompress.

Toy Museum (Spielzeugmuseum) – A Delight For All Ages

Nuremberg has long been regarded as the **"Toy Capital of the World"**, and nowhere is this legacy more vividly preserved than in the **Spielzeugmuseum (Toy Museum)**. Established in 1971, the museum showcases over **600 years of toy-making history**, demonstrating how playtime has evolved across centuries.

What You'll Discover Inside:

- **Antique Wooden Toys:** The museum holds an **extensive collection of handcrafted wooden toys from the 16th to 19th centuries** when Nuremberg was a hub for wooden dollhouses, miniature kitchens, and wind-up figurines.

- **Tin Toys and Model Trains:** One of the most impressive sections features the tin toy boom of the 19th and early 20th centuries, including rare pieces from manufacturers like **Lehmann and Bing**.

- **Teddy Bears and Dolls:** Step into the world of vintage **Steiff teddy bears, porcelain dolls, and detailed dollhouses**, some dating back over 200 years.

- **Modern Playthings:** The museum also celebrates **LEGO, Barbie, Playmobil, and electronic games**, showing how childhood entertainment has evolved in recent decades.

- **Interactive Play Area:** Children (and playful adults!) can enjoy a **hands-on experience** in a dedicated playroom filled with toys inspired by different eras.

Why It's a Must-Visit: Nuremberg's toy industry **helped shape childhood experiences worldwide**, and this museum offers a nostalgic, educational, and hands-on journey through that history. Whether you're an adult reminiscing about childhood favorites or a child seeing antique toys for the first time, **this museum creates a magical bridge between generations**.

Insider Tip: Head to the museum's **outdoor play area** on a sunny day—kids can try out traditional wooden toys while adults soak in the historic surroundings.

Memorium Nuremberg Trials – A Legacy Of Justice

Few places in the world hold as much legal and historical significance as the site of the Nuremberg Trials. Located inside the Palace of Justice, the Memorium Nuremberg Trials museum is dedicated to the groundbreaking trials that redefined international law following World War II.

Exploring the Museum:

- **Room 600 – The Historic Courtroom:** The very place where Nazi leaders faced justice between 1945 and 1946 remains largely intact. A visit here is nothing short of profound.

- **Multimedia Exhibits:** Interactive displays allow visitors to **watch original trial footage, hear survivor testimonies, and analyze key legal arguments** that laid the groundwork for modern international law.

- **The Birth of Human Rights Law:** The museum details how the trials led to the creation of the International Criminal Court (ICC) and the United Nations' Universal Declaration of Human Rights.

- **Profiles of the Defendants and Prosecutors:** Learn about the roles played by key figures, from **Hermann Göring to Chief Prosecutor Robert H. Jackson**, and the precedents they set for justice worldwide.

- **Ongoing Impact:** The museum explores modern war crimes tribunals, drawing direct connections between **Nuremberg's legacy and cases from Rwanda, the Balkans, and beyond.**

Why It's a Must-Visit: This is not just a museum—it's **a lesson in history, ethics, and the enduring importance of accountability.** The Nuremberg Trials set a precedent that continues to shape legal systems worldwide, and standing in Courtroom 600 is an unforgettable, humbling experience.

Insider Tip

If you want a **truly immersive experience**, visit on a **weekend when guided tours** are offered. The insights provided by experts add incredible depth to the exhibits.

Db Museum (German Railway Museum) – A Train Lover's Paradise

For those fascinated by locomotives and engineering marvels, the DB Museum (Deutsches Bahn Museum) is a must-visit. Opened in 1899, this is Germany's oldest railway museum, tracing the country's impressive rail history from the first steam engines to the high-speed ICE trains of today.

Highlights of the Museum:

DB Museum

- **The "Adler" – Germany's First Train:** The museum's crown jewel is the **original 1835 Adler locomotive**, the very first steam train to operate in Germany.

- **Historic Carriages:** From **royal train coaches used by German emperors** to **post-war locomotives**, each train car tells a unique story about different eras of German rail travel.

- **Model Railways:** An incredible collection of **detailed model railways**, including interactive displays where visitors can operate miniature train sets.

- **Modern Railway Innovations:** Learn how Germany has **pioneered cutting-edge train technology**, from the early electric locomotives to today's ultra-fast Intercity Express (ICE) trains.

- **Children's Railway Adventure Area:** A hands-on space where kids can **climb inside train carriages, operate levers, and explore the inner workings of locomotives**.

Why It's a Must-Visit: This museum is a **dream destination for train enthusiasts and

engineering fans alike. With its meticulously maintained locomotives, **rich history of railway expansion, and interactive exhibits**, the DB Museum offers an in-depth look at how Germany's railways have shaped both national and European transportation.

Insider Tip

If you're visiting with kids, don't miss the **Kinder-Bahnland**, an engaging play area where young visitors can drive their miniature trains through interactive landscapes.

Each of these museums offers a completely different yet equally fascinating experience, making them must-visit spots on any itinerary. Whether you're revisiting childhood memories at the Toy Museum, standing in the courtroom that changed history at the Memorium Nuremberg Trials, or geeking out over locomotives at the DB Museum, Nuremberg's museums promise deep insights, nostalgia, and unforgettable moments.

Chapter 7

Outdoor Activities & Nature Escapes

A city rich in culture and history, Nuremberg has more to offer than just museums and architectural wonders. There is a sanctuary for adventurers and nature lovers beyond its medieval walls. Nuremberg offers a wealth of outdoor activities and green places ideal for rest, discovery, and reestablishing a connection with nature, ranging from serene riverbanks to strenuous hiking paths. The area provides a variety of sceneries and outdoor experiences, whether you're looking for a tranquil getaway from the city's old streets or an exhilarating adventure. This chapter explores Nuremberg's top hiking paths, picturesque walks, verdant parks, cycling routes, and boating excursions.

Hiking Trails & Scenic Walks Near Nuremberg

Hiking the Franconian Switzerland (Fränkische Schweiz) Trails One of the most breathtaking regions near Nuremberg, Franconian Switzerland is a paradise for hikers. Characterized by dramatic limestone cliffs, deep valleys, and picturesque villages, this region boasts over **6,500 kilometers of marked trails**. Notable routes include:

- **Riesenburg Loop:** A moderate trail leading to the Riesenburg natural rock formation, which offers panoramic views of the rolling hills and dense forests.

- **Püttlachtal Trail:** A picturesque hike along the Püttlach River, famous for its serene ambiance and quaint half-timbered houses.

- **Castle Trail (Burgenweg):** Connects several medieval castles, such as *Pottenstein Castle* and *Egloffstein Castle*, offering a blend of history and nature.

- **Maximiliansgrotte Trail:** A fantastic route leading to the stunning *Maximilian's Cave*, known for its impressive stalactites and stalagmites.

Pegnitz River Trail – A Riverside Escape For those seeking a more relaxed nature walk, the **Pegnitz River Trail** provides a scenic route along the gently flowing river. This picturesque trail is perfect for a leisurely walk, run, or a family-friendly excursion.

Püttlachtal Trail

- **Highlights of the Trail:** Beautiful **bridges, lush meadows**, and **secluded picnic spots**.
- **Wildlife Watching:** Spot kingfishers, herons, and even beavers along the riverbanks.
- **Marienberg Park Connection:** This trail conveniently connects to Marienberg Park, one

of Nuremberg's largest green spaces, ideal for a longer nature escape.

Reichswald Forest – A Tranquil Getaway
Southeast of Nuremberg lies the **Reichswald Forest**, a vast natural expanse offering numerous hiking and cycling trails. This historic forest was once a royal hunting ground and remains a favorite among outdoor enthusiasts today.

- **Reichswald Circular Trail: A moderate-level hike** through dense beech and pine forests, with occasional clearings revealing historic bunkers and old sandstone quarries.

- **Autumn & Spring Beauty:** The forest comes alive with a riot of colors in autumn, while spring brings a fresh burst of green and blooming wildflowers.

- **Wildlife Spotting:** Home to deer, foxes, and various bird species, this forest is a haven for nature lovers and photographers.

Best Parks & Gardens in the City

Hesperidengärten (Hesperides Gardens) – A Baroque Botanical Gem Nestled in Nuremberg's St. Johannis district, these gardens date back to the 17th century and were once part of aristocratic homes.

- **Citrus Groves:** The gardens are named after the golden apples of Greek mythology, reflected in the many citrus trees that bloom here.

- **Ornate Statues & Fountains:** Delicately sculpted statues and classical fountains dot the landscape, offering a serene escape within the city.

- **Ideal for a Leisurely Stroll:** Shaded benches, symmetrical paths, and blooming flora make this a perfect retreat from the city's hustle.

Stadtpark (City Park) – A Green Oasis One of Nuremberg's most beloved parks, **Stadtpark** offers vast green spaces and well-maintained paths for walking, jogging, and cycling.

- **Spring & Summer Blooms:** In the warmer months, the park is adorned with seasonal flower displays, making it a delightful sight for visitors.

- **Peaceful Ponds & Sculptures:** The park features ponds filled with swans and ducks, complemented by impressive sculptures that enhance the tranquil atmosphere.

- **Picnic Areas & Outdoor Cafés:** Perfect for a lazy afternoon, Stadtpark provides plenty of space to relax with a book or enjoy a picnic under shady trees.

Cycling Routes & Bike Tours

The Pegnitz River Cycling Route Cycling along the **Pegnitz River** is an enjoyable way to see Nuremberg's scenic beauty.

- **Distance:** The route extends **35 kilometers**, passing through picturesque landscapes, charming towns, and historic sites.

- **Beer Gardens & Rest Stops:** Traditional **beer gardens dot the route**, offering a refreshing break with local Bavarian specialties.

- **Wildlife Watching:** Keep an eye out for **herons, kingfishers, and beavers** along the riverbanks.

Franconian Lake District Route For a longer cycling adventure, the **Franconian Lake District** offers picturesque lakeside rides.

- **Highlights:** Explore the beautiful *Brombachsee* and *Altmühlsee* lakes, ideal for a combination of cycling and water sports.

- **Family-Friendly Paths:** The relatively flat terrain makes this a great option for families looking to enjoy a leisurely ride.

- **Water Sports & Rest Stops:** Stop by one of the many lakeside beer gardens and enjoy a Bavarian meal with a view.

Boating on the Pegnitz River

Canoeing & Kayaking Adventures

- Join a **guided canoe tour** along the Pegnitz River, exploring its winding waterways and hidden pockets of wildlife.

- Paddle through the **historical Old Town**, where medieval bridges and half-timbered houses line the riverbanks.

- Experienced kayakers can venture further into **Pegnitzauen**, a natural paradise perfect for spotting herons, ducks, and even otters.

Traditional Raft Rides For a more relaxed water experience, hop on a traditional **flat-bottomed raft tour**, an old practice that dates back centuries.

- Local guides share stories of Nuremberg's **history, legends, and the river's significance** in trade and transportation.

- Sunset rides offer a breathtaking view of the city's medieval skyline as the waters shimmer in the golden light.

- Some tours include onboard drinks and local delicacies, making for a unique way to explore the city.

Insider Tip: A Secret Riverside Spot for Tranquility If you want to escape the crowds and find a peaceful spot by the Pegnitz, head to Hainberg Nature Reserve. A hidden treasure just outside Nuremberg, this nature reserve offers serene walking paths, untouched woodlands, and opportunities to spot local wildlife, making it the perfect place to unwind and connect with nature. Pack a picnic, bring a good book, and soak in the tranquility away from the tourist crowds.

Chapter 8

Food & Drinks – A Culinary Journey

Nuremberg is not just a city of historical landmarks and medieval charm; it is also a paradise for food lovers. From its world-famous sausages to its centuries-old gingerbread tradition, Nuremberg's culinary scene is a delicious blend of tradition, quality, and innovation. Whether you're indulging in a classic Nürnberger Rostbratwurst, savoring a Michelin-starred meal, or exploring the vibrant local markets, this chapter will take you on an unforgettable culinary journey.

Must-Try Local Dishes (Bratwurst, Lebkuchen & More)

Nürnberger Rostbratwurst – The Iconic Sausage

Nuremberg's bratwurst is legendary. These small, thin sausages, measuring about 9 cm long, have been made according to a strict recipe for over 700 years. The key to their unique taste lies in the finely ground pork, marjoram, and a special smoking process. Traditionally, they are grilled over a beechwood fire and served three at a time on a fresh roll (Drei im Weggla) or with sauerkraut and mustard on a plate. The best place to try them? Historic sausage kitchens like Bratwursthäusle or Bratwurst Röslein.

Nürnberger Rostbratwurst

Lebkuchen – Nuremberg's World-Famous Gingerbread

No visit to Nuremberg is complete without tasting its famous Lebkuchen. This soft, spiced gingerbread has been a local specialty since the 14th century, originally baked by Franconian monks. Traditional Nuremberg Lebkuchen is made with honey, nuts, candied fruit, and a blend of warming spices like cinnamon and cloves. The best variety is the Elisenlebkuchen, which contains a high percentage of nuts and little to no flour. Visit Lebkuchen-Schmidt or Wicklein to sample authentic handmade versions.

Schäufele – Franconian Pork Shoulder

Schäufele

Schäufele is a must-try for meat lovers. This roasted pork shoulder dish is a Franconian delicacy, slow-cooked until the meat is tender and topped with crispy, golden-brown crackling. It is typically served with potato dumplings and rich gravy, making it a hearty and satisfying meal.

Blaue Zipfel – A Unique Sausage Dish

Unlike the grilled Nürnberger Rostbratwurst, Blaue Zipfel is a tangy, vinegar-infused sausage dish. The sausages are simmered in a broth of vinegar, onions, white wine, and spices, giving them a distinctive sour flavor. It's best enjoyed with fresh bread and a cold Franconian beer.

Fränkischer Sauerbraten

Fränkischer Sauerbraten – Bavaria's Marinated Pot Roast

Sauerbraten is a slow-cooked beef dish marinated in a mixture of vinegar, wine, and spices for several days. The result is a tender and flavorful pot roast, often served with red cabbage and potato dumplings. Each Franconian family has its variation of the recipe, making it a beloved local specialty.

Fine Dining & Michelin-Starred Restaurants

Essigbrätl's

One of the oldest and most prestigious restaurants in Nuremberg, Essigbrätl's offers a sophisticated take on traditional Franconian cuisine. Their menu highlights locally sourced ingredients, expertly prepared dishes, and an extensive wine selection, making it a top choice for fine dining.

Restaurant ZweiSinn Meiers

Holding a Michelin star, ZweiSinn Meiers blends fine dining with a modern bistro atmosphere. The restaurant is known for its creative fusion of French and Franconian flavors, offering dishes like venison with lingonberries and truffle-infused potato foam.

Waidwerk

A true gem for gastronomes, Waidwerk has earned a Michelin star for its seasonal and artistic approach to Bavarian cuisine. With dishes like smoked char with pickled vegetables and wild herbs, every meal here is an elegant culinary adventure.

C'est la Vie

For those who crave a taste of France in Nuremberg, C'est la Vie delivers exceptional French fine dining. The menu features delicate seafood dishes, refined sauces, and impeccable wine pairings, making it one of the most exquisite dining experiences in the city.

Tisane

If you're looking for an intimate dining experience, Tisane is a hidden treasure. With a focus on organic and seasonal ingredients, the chef's tasting menu is a masterclass in balancing flavors and textures.

Best Traditional Bavarian Beer Gardens

Nuremberg's beer gardens are more than just places to drink—they're social hubs steeped in tradition, where locals and visitors alike gather to enjoy exceptional brews and hearty meals under the open sky.

Hausbrauerei Altstadthof – A Historic Brewery Experience

Located in the heart of the Old Town, Hausbrauerei Altstadthof is renowned for its handcrafted red beer (Rotbier), a Nuremberg specialty. This charming beer garden offers a cozy, traditional atmosphere where you can sip on organic, house-brewed beers while feasting on Franconian specialties like Nürnberger Rostbratwurst and Obatzda, a Bavarian cheese delicacy.

Biergarten im Hexenhäusle – A Rustic Hideaway

Tucked away near Nuremberg Castle, Hexenhäusle offers an intimate beer garden experience surrounded by lush greenery. With wooden benches, lantern-lit evenings, and an impressive selection of local brews, this spot is perfect for those seeking an authentic Bavarian experience. Be sure to try their Schäufele (pork shoulder), a Franconian classic that pairs perfectly with a crisp lager.

Hausbrauerei Altstadthof

Gutmann am Dutzendteich – A Lakeside Retreat

For a beer garden with a view, head to Gutmann am Dutzendteich, overlooking the serene Dutzendteich Lake. This spacious establishment serves one of the best Weissbiers (wheat beers) in the city, brewed by the famous Gutmann Brewery. Pair it with a traditional pretzel and Obatzda for the full Bavarian experience.

Street Food & Casual Dining Spots

For a taste of Nuremberg's fast and flavorful street food scene, you don't have to look far. Whether you're strolling through the Hauptmarkt or exploring local festivals, these must-try bites will satisfy your cravings.

Nürnberger Rostbratwurst – The Iconic Sausage

No visit to Nuremberg is complete without trying the city's world-famous Nürnberger Rostbratwurst. These small, flavorful sausages are traditionally grilled over a beechwood fire and served three at a time in a bun (Drei im Weckla). Head to the Bratwursthäusle or a street vendor near the Hauptmarkt for an authentic taste.

Lebkuchen – The Sweet Side of Nuremberg

Known worldwide as the birthplace of Lebkuchen (gingerbread), Nuremberg offers an array of deliciously spiced cookies that date back to the Middle

Ages. For the best Lebkuchen, visit Schmidt Lebkuchen, where you can sample classic flavors like honey-almond and chocolate-dipped varieties.

Food Stalls at the Hauptmarkt

Hauptmarkt, the city's main square, is a fantastic spot for discovering local street food. Depending on the season, you'll find fresh pretzels, warm mulled wine (during winter), and regional cheeses. Keep an eye out for seasonal delicacies, especially during the world-famous Christkindlesmarkt.

Kokoro – A Fusion Twist

For an alternative street food experience, Kokoro is a must-visit. This Japanese street food spot offers everything from bao buns to ramen bowls, giving visitors a break from traditional Franconian fare.

Vegetarian & Vegan Options in Nuremberg

Gone are the days when Bavarian cuisine was all about meat-heavy dishes. Nuremberg has embraced plant-based dining, offering numerous vegetarian and vegan-friendly restaurants that showcase creativity and fresh ingredients.

Herr Lenz – A Vegan Paradise

Located in the trendy Gostenhof district, Herr Lenz is a cozy vegan bistro known for its delicious plant-based burgers, homemade cakes, and freshly brewed organic coffee. Their seitan schnitzel and vegan currywurst are particularly popular among locals.

Etage – Modern and Sustainable

Frittenwerk

Etage is a stylish café that focuses on sustainability and locally sourced ingredients. Their rotating menu includes dishes like vegan pumpkin risotto, tofu stir-fry, and an excellent selection of fresh smoothies and cold-pressed juices.

Frittenwerk – Gourmet Fries & Vegan Dips

If you're in the mood for something casual yet satisfying, Frittenwerk specializes in loaded fries with creative toppings, including several vegan options like avocado-lime sauce and plant-based cheese. It's an excellent spot for a quick, flavorful bite.

Hempels Burger – Plant-Based Burgers Done Right

Hempels Burger offers a dedicated vegetarian and vegan menu, featuring everything from lentil-based patties to beyond meat burgers. The sweet potato fries and homemade vegan aioli are crowd favorites.

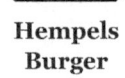

Hempels Burger

While Nuremberg's culinary scene offers everything from street food to Michelin-starred dining, one of the best ways to explore its flavors is through a guided food tour. Companies like Nuremberg Food Walk offer immersive tasting experiences, leading you through historic markets, bakeries, and hidden gastronomic gems.

If you want to experience Nuremberg's food scene like a local, time your visit around one of the city's culinary events. The Nuremberg Bierfest, held every summer, is a fantastic opportunity to sample local craft beers and Bavarian delicacies, while the Christkindlesmarkt in winter is an unmissable treat for food lovers, with its array of seasonal delights like mulled wine, roasted almonds, and traditional sausages.

Map Showing various Restaurants in Nuremberg

Chapter 9

Nuremberg's Nightlife & Entertainment

As the sun sets, Nuremberg's historic streets transform into a vibrant playground for night owls. Whether you're looking for a cozy pub to sip on Franconian beer, a live music venue pulsing with energy, or a sophisticated cultural performance, the city offers an eclectic mix of after-dark experiences. From the buzzing bars of the Old Town to hidden speakeasies and atmospheric theaters, Nuremberg's nightlife scene caters to every mood. This chapter takes you through the best spots to experience the city at night, with a mix of local favorites and unforgettable venues.

Best Bars & Pubs for a Great Night Out

Nuremberg's bar scene blends historic charm with modern mixology, offering everything from centuries-old beer taverns to trendy cocktail lounges.

Traditional Beer Halls & Pubs

- **Hausbrauerei Altstadthof** – This microbrewery in the heart of the Old Town is the best place to try Nuremberg's signature Rotbier (red beer). The rustic wooden interiors and vaulted cellar provide a warm, authentic atmosphere.

Zum Gulden Stern

- **Zum Gulden Stern** – Germany's oldest bratwurst restaurant is not just about food—it also serves fantastic local beers in a setting that dates back to 1419.

- **Barfüßer Hausbrauerei** – A lively brewery that pairs its house-brewed beers with traditional Franconian dishes, perfect for a relaxed yet vibrant evening.

Cocktail Bars & Lounges

- **Gelbes Haus** – A speakeasy-style cocktail bar with a hidden entrance, offering expertly crafted drinks in an intimate setting.

Die Rote Bar

- **Die Rote Bar** – A stylish venue with a theatrical red-themed interior and a stellar cocktail menu that leans heavily on creativity.

- **Kontiki** – A tropical oasis in the middle of the city, serving tiki-style cocktails and exotic rum blends.

Rooftop & Wine Bars

- **Skybar Nuremberg** – Perched atop the city, this bar offers panoramic views, chic decor, and a refined wine selection.

- **Weinstock** – A charming wine bar with an extensive selection of regional Franconian wines, ideal for a quieter, more refined night out.

Live Music Venues & Concert Halls

Nuremberg has a thriving music scene, with venues catering to everything from jazz to rock and electronic beats.

Intimate Jazz & Blues Clubs

- **Jazz Studio Nürnberg** – A legendary underground jazz club where local and international musicians perform in an intimate, candlelit setting.

- **Hirsch** – A staple in Nuremberg's music scene, featuring a mix of blues, indie, and rock performances.

Large-Scale Concert Halls & Arenas

- **Meistersingerhalle** – Nuremberg's premier concert venue, hosting everything from classical performances to international pop and rock artists.

- **Max-Morlock-Stadion** – While mainly a football stadium, it occasionally transforms into a massive concert arena for global music icons.

- **Löwensaal** – A historic venue known for its diverse lineup of concerts, from alternative rock to electronic music events.

Underground & Alternative Music Spaces

- **Z-Bau** – An artistic and cultural hub that regularly hosts underground and indie music acts.

- **Stereo Club** – Known for its electronic beats and alternative club nights, attracting both local and international DJs.

Theater & Cultural Performances

For those who enjoy a refined night out, Nuremberg offers exceptional theater productions, opera, and cultural showcases.

Classic & Modern Theater

- **Staatstheater Nürnberg** – The city's premier theater, featuring world-class opera, ballet, and drama performances.

- **Theater Pfütze** – A small but highly regarded venue known for its experimental and contemporary plays.

- **Gostner Hoftheater** – A hidden gem focusing on avant-garde and alternative theater productions.

Opera & Classical Performances

- **Nuremberg Symphony Orchestra** – One of Germany's most renowned orchestras, performing at the Meistersingerhalle.

- **Pocket Opera Nürnberg** – A unique initiative offering intimate opera experiences in smaller, unconventional venues.

Unique Nighttime Experiences in Nuremberg

Staatstheater Nürnberg

Beyond the bars and theaters, Nuremberg has plenty of unexpected and immersive nighttime activities.

Historic & Haunted Tours

- **Nightwatchman Tour** – Step back in time and explore Nuremberg's medieval past with a guide dressed as a traditional nightwatchman.

- **Ghost Tour of Nuremberg** – A spine-chilling journey through the city's darker history, including legends of haunted alleyways and eerie medieval executions.

Late-Night Museum Visits

- **Germanisches Nationalmuseum Night Sessions** – On special occasions, this vast museum extends its hours for themed late-night events.

- **Albrecht Dürer House by Night** – Experience the home of the Renaissance artist in a candlelit atmosphere.

Late-Night Food Adventures

- **Bratwursthäusle Midnight Grill** – Some of the best bratwursts in town, available even after the bars close.

- **Nuremberg Christmas Market at Night** – If visiting in December, the Christkindlesmarkt is a magical evening destination with twinkling lights and warm mulled wine.

Insider Tip

For a truly unique night out, book a table at **Gelbes Haus**, one of Nuremberg's best hidden speakeasies. After an evening of cocktails, end the night at **Barfüßer Hausbrauerei**, where you can sip on freshly brewed beer in a historic beer hall that dates back centuries. Want a touch of adventure? Join a **Nightwatchman Tour** to explore Nuremberg's eerie past by lantern light.

Chapter 10

Shopping in Nuremberg

In addition to its medieval beauty and historical sites, Nuremberg is a shopping haven for those seeking a blend of upscale stores, lively marketplaces, and traditional craftsmanship. The city offers something for every taste, whether you wish to indulge in upscale shopping, discover undiscovered artisan treasures, or bring home a bit of Nuremberg's rich history. From genuine souvenirs to chic retail avenues and upscale stores, we'll walk you through the greatest shopping experiences Nuremberg has to offer in this chapter.

Where to Buy Authentic Nuremberg Souvenirs

If you want to bring home a piece of Nuremberg's culture, the city is brimming with unique souvenirs that tell a story. From traditional crafts to famous edible delights, here are the best places to find authentic Nuremberg keepsakes.

Lebkuchen Schmidt: The Home of Nuremberg Gingerbread

Bratwurstglöcklein

No visit to Nuremberg is complete without trying its world-famous Lebkuchen (gingerbread). Lebkuchen Schmidt is the most renowned purveyor, offering beautifully decorated tins filled with deliciously spiced gingerbread cookies. These make the perfect gift or personal treat to savor long after your trip.

Handmade Wooden Crafts at the Nuremberg Christmas Market

If you're visiting during the holiday season, the Christkindlesmarkt is the ultimate destination for traditional wooden crafts, nutcrackers, and handcrafted Christmas ornaments. Many of these items are made in the nearby Erzgebirge region, famous for its woodworking traditions.

Bratwurstglöcklein: Take-Home Nuremberg Sausages

For food lovers, vacuum-packed Nuremberg bratwurst from Bratwurstglöcklein is a must. This specialty shop ensures that you can enjoy the city's beloved sausages even after you leave.

German Pewter Figurines & Tankards at Zinnfiguren-Zentrum

Collectors and history enthusiasts will appreciate the beautifully crafted pewter figurines available at Zinnfiguren-Zentrum. These hand-painted miniatures depict scenes from Nuremberg's past, making them a distinctive and historical souvenir.

Best Shopping Streets & Markets

Nuremberg boasts a variety of shopping districts, each offering a different retail experience. Whether you prefer large department stores, independent boutiques, or vibrant markets, here's where to go for the best shopping experience.

Karolinenstraße: The Heart of Nuremberg's Retail Scene

Karolinenstraße is the city's main shopping artery, packed with popular international brands, large department stores, and flagship outlets. It's the go-to destination for everything from clothing to electronics, offering a blend of modern retail convenience in a historic setting.

Kaiserstraße: Upscale Shopping & Designer Brands

For those with a taste for luxury, Kaiserstraße is where you'll find high-end fashion boutiques, exclusive jewelry stores, and designer brands. This elegant street exudes sophistication, attracting shoppers looking for premium-quality goods.

Hauptmarkt: The Soul of Nuremberg's Market Culture

The Hauptmarkt is famous for hosting the Christkindlesmarkt in winter, but it remains a bustling marketplace year-round. Here, you can shop for fresh produce, local delicacies, flowers, and handcrafted goods. It's also the best place to sample Nuremberg's culinary delights before buying them as souvenirs.

Craft Markets & Flea Markets for Hidden Treasures

Nuremberg's artisanal markets and flea markets offer a treasure trove of vintage finds, handcrafted items, and antiques. The Trempelmarkt, held twice a year, is the largest flea market in southern Germany and an excellent place to discover unique collectibles.

Heinemann

Luxury Boutiques & Local Artisan Shops

For those seeking exclusive shopping experiences, Nuremberg offers a mix of high-end boutiques and locally owned artisan shops that showcase exceptional craftsmanship.

Heinemann: The Finest Jewelry & Watches

Heinemann is one of the city's most prestigious jewelers, offering exquisite watches, diamond-studded pieces, and bespoke designs. If you're looking for a timeless souvenir, this is the place to find it.

Leder Wolf: Premium Handmade Leather Goods

Leder Wolf specializes in handcrafted leather products, from stylish bags to custom-made belts. Each piece is a testament to the skill of local artisans who have mastered traditional leatherworking techniques.

Porzellan Manufaktur Nymphenburg: Fine Bavarian Porcelain

For lovers of elegant home decor, Nymphenburg's porcelain collections are a must-see. These exquisite, hand-painted pieces are perfect for those who appreciate timeless luxury and craftsmanship.

Kunsthandwerkerhof: A Hidden Village of Artisans

Located within the historic city walls, the Kunsthandwerkerhof is a charming enclave of small workshops where artisans create and sell handmade pottery, glassware, and traditional German crafts. This is the ideal spot to find one-of-a-kind items and watch skilled craftsmen at work.

Christmas Markets: A Winter Wonderland

Nuremberg, a city steeped in medieval charm, comes alive with a magical glow during the Christmas season. Famous for hosting one of the most renowned Christmas markets in the world, the Nuremberg

Christkindlesmarkt, the city transforms into a festive wonderland, radiating warmth, tradition, and the irresistible scent of roasted almonds and mulled wine. However, the seasonal enchantment doesn't stop there—Nuremberg and its surrounding areas boast a variety of Christmas markets, each with a unique character and atmosphere. From charming historic squares to hidden gems brimming with handcrafted treasures, this chapter explores the best Christmas markets and winter festivities in and around Nuremberg, ensuring an unforgettable holiday experience.

The Legendary Christkindlesmarkt – Nuremberg's Crown Jewel

There are Christmas markets, and then there is the **Nuremberg Christkindlesmarkt**, one of the oldest and most celebrated in the world. Dating back to **at least 1628**, this market is steeped in history and tradition, drawing over **two million visitors** each year.

- **Location:** Hauptmarkt Square, in front of the iconic **Church of Our Lady (Frauenkirche).**

- **Christkind Opening Ceremony:** Every year, on the **Friday before the first Advent**, the famous **Christkind (Christmas Angel)**, dressed in a golden robe with a flowing crown, opens the market from the church balcony, welcoming visitors with a poetic prologue.

- **Glühwein & Nuremberg Sausages:** A visit isn't complete without sipping on a steaming cup of **Nuremberg's famous mulled wine (Glühwein)** and tasting the city's iconic **Nürnberger Rostbratwurst**, which has been a local specialty for centuries.

- **Handmade Treasures:** Over **180 stalls** offer beautifully crafted goods, from intricate wooden ornaments and nutcrackers to hand-poured beeswax candles and delicate glass baubles.

Sister Market: The Sister Cities Market

Just a short walk from the main Christkindlesmarkt, this hidden gem is a cultural delight.

- **International Flair:** Booths from Nuremberg's sister cities—from **Nice (France) to Glasgow (Scotland) and San Carlos (Nicaragua)**—bring global holiday traditions to the heart of Nuremberg.

- **Global Crafts & Treats:** Sample delicious **Scottish whisky, Czech pastries, and handmade toys from Nicaragua**.

- **Exclusive Finds:** The market offers unique, international Christmas gifts that you won't find anywhere else in the city.

Handwerkerhof – The Medieval Christmas Experience

For those seeking a glimpse into Nuremberg's medieval past, the **Handwerkerhof Christmas Market** is a must-visit. This tiny, fairy-tale-like village inside the city's old walls transforms into a magical scene with twinkling lanterns, half-timbered houses, and artisans showcasing their craftsmanship.

- **Handmade Crafts:** Explore stalls selling traditional **hand-painted pewter figurines, wooden toys, and artisan Christmas pyramids.**

- **Sizzling Bratwurst & Local Beer:** Sample the city's world-famous **Nürnberger Rostbratwurst**, traditionally grilled over an open beechwood fire, and pair it with a locally brewed beer.

- **Medieval Performances:** Enjoy live demonstrations by blacksmiths, glassblowers, and candle makers, bringing old-world craftsmanship to life.

The Children's Christmas Market – A Magical Experience

Children will find **Hans-Sachs-Platz** transformed into a festive playground, tailor-made for little ones to revel in Christmas magic.

- **The Christmas Bakery:** A delightful space where children can bake and decorate their gingerbread (Lebkuchen).

- **Carousels & Mini-Train Rides:** Traditional rides offer fun for the little ones, complete with a chance to meet the Christkind.

- **Wish Angel House:** Kids can write letters to Christkind, expressing their holiday wishes and posting them in a special golden mailbox.

Kaiserburg Castle Christmas Illumination Walk

The historic **Kaiserburg Castle**, perched on a hill overlooking Nuremberg, is even more enchanting in winter.

- **Magical Views:** Snow-covered rooftops and twinkling lights make for an awe-inspiring panorama of the old town.

- **Winter Castle Tours:** Learn about the **Holy Roman Empire**, the castle's medieval history, and its strategic importance.

- **Romantic Strolls:** The illuminated castle grounds offer a dreamy evening walk, perfect for couples and photographers alike.

Historic Markets Beyond the City Center

Erlangen Christmas Market

Located just **30 minutes from Nuremberg**, this smaller, cozier market offers a more relaxed and local feel, with a focus on traditional crafts and regional specialties.

- **Specialty Stalls:** Artisanal chocolates, handmade woolen garments, and Franconian delicacies like **Küchle (fried dough pastries).**

- **Outdoor Ice Skating Rink:** Open for all ages, offering festive fun against a backdrop of twinkling lights.

- **Fire Pits & Live Music:** Enjoy the warmth of open fire pits while listening to traditional Christmas carols performed by local musicians.

Boating on the Pegnitz River

One of the most serene outdoor experiences in Nuremberg is exploring the **Pegnitz River** by boat. Whether you opt for a relaxing **paddle boat ride** or a guided tour, the views of the Old Town and its charming half-timbered houses are breathtaking.

- **Canoeing & Kayaking:** Paddle along the calm waters of the Pegnitz, passing through historic districts and under picturesque bridges.

- **Boat Tours:** Several companies offer boat tours, where knowledgeable guides narrate the city's rich history and architecture.

- **Best Viewing Spot:** The **Fleisch Bridge** offers one of the most picturesque views of the Pegnitz River and is a must-visit at sunset.

Insider Tip

If you're looking for truly unique souvenirs, visit the workshops in the Handwerkerhof (Craftsmen's Courtyard), where you can see artisans creating hand-blown glass, leather goods, and wooden toys. Many of these items are not available anywhere else, making them rare finds that encapsulate Nuremberg's craftsmanship.

Discover Nuremberg's Hidden Winter Garden While the popular Christmas markets are a must-visit, avoid the biggest crowds by heading to the Hexenhäusle (Witch's Cottage) Beer Garden, nestled near the castle. This charming, lesser-known spot serves warm mulled wine (Glühwein), hearty Franconian dishes, and delicious homemade strudel in a cozy, fairytale setting. It's the perfect place to warm up on a chilly winter day while enjoying an authentic slice of Nuremberg's winter magic.

Chapter 11

7 Must-Do Things in Nuremberg

The city of Nuremberg is rich in culture, history, and unusual experiences. The city provides a wide range of activities that highlight its attractiveness, whether you're a history buff, foodie, or someone looking for an amazing adventure. These are the top seven things visitors to Nuremberg just must do to make a lasting impression.

1. Explore Nuremberg Castle: A Journey Through Time

Perched atop a sandstone ridge, **Nuremberg Castle** is a testament to the city's medieval grandeur. This fortress, which once housed Holy Roman Emperors, offers breathtaking panoramic views over the Old Town.

- **Imperial Palace:** Walk through the Kaiserburg's grand halls, where emperors once ruled.

- **Deep Well:** This 50-meter-deep well has been an essential part of the castle's defenses for centuries.

- **Sinwell Tower:** Climbing this tower rewards you with sweeping views of Nuremberg's rooftops.

Why It's a Must: The castle is an architectural masterpiece that brings history to life, making it an unmissable stop.

2. Stroll Through the Historic Old Town (Altstadt)

Nuremberg's **Altstadt** is a fairytale setting, featuring half-timbered houses, cobbled streets, and iconic landmarks. The city's medieval charm is best experienced by taking a leisurely walk through this beautifully preserved district.

- **Hauptmarkt:** Home to the world-famous Christkindlesmarkt during Christmas, this square is vibrant year-round.

- **Schöner Brunnen (Beautiful Fountain):** A 14th-century Gothic fountain with a golden ring that is said to bring good luck when turned.

- **Weißgerbergasse:** This picturesque street, lined with traditional craftsmen's houses, is a perfect spot for photography.

Why It's a Must: The Altstadt is the beating heart of Nuremberg, offering an immersive historical experience with every step.

3. Visit the Documentation Center Nazi Party Rally Grounds

For those interested in history, the **Documentation Center** provides an in-depth look at Nuremberg's role during the Third Reich. The museum, located in the former Nazi rally grounds, features exhibits on propaganda, the rise of the Nazi party, and the aftermath of World War II.

- **Great Hall:** A partially completed coliseum-style building that was intended to glorify the Nazi regime.

- **Path of Remembrance:** An outdoor walking tour through the remains of the Nazi rally sites.

- **Permanent Exhibition:** Features first-hand accounts and multimedia displays.

Why It's a Must: Understanding history is key to preventing its repetition, and this site provides a powerful and educational experience.

4. Indulge in Traditional Nuremberg Bratwurst

A trip to Nuremberg isn't complete without tasting its legendary **Nürnberger Bratwurst**. These small, flavorful sausages have been a local delicacy for over 700 years.

- **Bratwursthäusle:** One of the oldest restaurants serving traditional bratwurst grilled over a beechwood fire.

- **Drei im Weggla:** A popular street food version—three bratwursts served in a crunchy roll with mustard.

- **Pair with Local Beer:** Franconian beer is the perfect companion to these savory sausages.

Why It's a Must: The flavor of a perfectly grilled Nürnberger Bratwurst is a culinary experience that embodies the city's heritage.

5. Marvel at the Gothic Beauty of St. Lorenz Church

The **St. Lorenz Church** is a striking Gothic cathedral with towering spires and stunning stained-glass windows. This church, which was heavily damaged during WWII and later restored, is a testament to Nuremberg's resilience.

- **The Lorenz Choir:** One of the most impressive choirs in Germany, performing sacred music.

- **The Angelic Salutation:** A magnificent wood carving by Veit Stoss, showcasing intricate artistry.

- **Organ Concerts:** Regular performances that fill the cathedral with breathtaking acoustics.

Why It's a Must: St. Lorenz Church is a masterpiece of Gothic architecture and a peaceful retreat from the bustling city.

6. Experience the Magic of the Nuremberg Christmas Market

If visiting in December, the **Christkindlesmarkt** is a dreamlike experience. This world-famous Christmas market transforms Nuremberg into a winter wonderland, attracting visitors from across the globe.

- **Handcrafted Ornaments:** Traditional wooden decorations and glass baubles make for perfect souvenirs.

- **Glühwein & Lebkuchen:** Sip on spiced mulled wine while savoring Nuremberg's famous gingerbread.

- **The Christkind:** A beloved figure who opens the market with a festive speech.

Why It's a Must: The Nuremberg Christmas Market is one of the most magical holiday experiences in the world, blending tradition, festivity, and culinary delights.

7. Take a Scenic Walk Along the Pegnitz River & City Walls

For a tranquil escape, walk along the **Pegnitz River**, where picturesque bridges and green parks provide a serene contrast to the historic city center.

- **Henkersteg (Hangman's Bridge):** A medieval wooden bridge with a haunting past.

- **Trödelmarkt:** A charming island in the river filled with boutique shops and cafés.

- **City Walls & Towers:** Explore the well-preserved fortifications that once protected the city.

Pegnitz River

Why It's a Must: The riverbanks and city walls offer a perfect blend of nature, history, and stunning views of Nuremberg.

Insider Tip: For a truly unique experience, visit the **Historische Felsengänge**, Nuremberg's underground rock-cut cellars. These tunnels, dating back to the Middle Ages, were used for beer storage and later served as bomb shelters during WWII. A guided tour reveals fascinating stories hidden beneath the city's surface!

Map Showing various Things to Do in Nuremberg

Chapter 12

Day Trips & Excursions from Nuremberg

In addition to being a destination in and of itself, Nuremberg serves as an ideal starting point for visits to some of Bavaria's most breathtaking and important historical sites. You can discover secret treasures tucked away in the heart of Franconia, tour UNESCO-listed heritage sites, and enter ancient towns frozen in time all within a short drive or train ride. These day trips from Nuremberg will enrich your vacation with amazing experiences, regardless of your interests in history, beautiful scenery, or genuine Bavarian culture.

Bamberg: The Little Venice Of Bavaria

Bamberg is often referred to as "Little Venice" due to its charming half-timbered houses lining the Regnitz River. This UNESCO-listed town is renowned for its well-preserved medieval architecture, winding cobblestone streets, and unique beer culture.

Bamberg

Altes Rathaus – The Iconic Town Hall is stretched dramatically in the middle of the Regnitz River, the Altes Rathaus (Old Town Hall) is one of Bamberg's most photographed landmarks. Legend has it that the bishop of Bamberg denied the townspeople land to build a town hall, so they constructed an artificial island and built it there instead. The result? A striking blend of Gothic and Baroque architecture with frescoes that appear to burst from the walls.

Bamberg Cathedral & The Tomb of Henry II

This stunning 13th-century cathedral is home to the only papal tomb in Germany. Inside, you'll find intricate sculptures, including the enigmatic Bamberg Horseman, a masterpiece that still puzzles historians today.

Bamberg's Beer Culture

Bamberg is famous for its Rauchbier, a smoked beer with a distinctive smoky aroma reminiscent of bacon. Visit Schlenkerla, the city's most famous brewery, where you can sample this unique brew straight from the wooden barrel.

Insider Tip: Visit the riverside district known as "Little Venice" at sunset for breathtaking views and a truly magical atmosphere.

Rothenburg Ob Der Tauber: A Fairytale Town

With its preserved medieval walls, cobblestone streets, and pastel-colored buildings, Rothenburg ob der Tauber feels like stepping into a fairytale. It is one of the best-preserved medieval towns in Germany and a must-visit for those who love history and photography.

Plönlein – The Most Famous View in Rothenburg

This postcard-perfect scene is what dreams are made of—a crooked timbered house flanked by two medieval towers, marking the entrance to the old town. It is easily one of the most photographed spots in Germany.

Medieval Crime and Punishment Museum

Dive into the eerie past of medieval justice with displays of torture devices, legal documents, and peculiar punishments used in the Middle Ages.

The Christmas Museum & Käthe Wohlfahrt Christmas Village

No matter the season, Rothenburg celebrates Christmas all year round! The Christmas Museum and Käthe Wohlfahrt Christmas Village offer festive ornaments and decorations that make for wonderful souvenirs.

Insider Tip: Stay until evening to see the town lit up in soft golden hues—it's a sight straight out of a storybook.

Regensburg: A Unesco Heritage Gem

Regensburg is one of Germany's oldest cities, boasting well-preserved Roman architecture and a lively old town filled with historical sites.

The Stone Bridge (Steinerne Brücke)

Built in the 12th century, this medieval bridge has stood the test of time and offers stunning views of the

Danube River. It was once a vital trade route connecting northern and southern Europe.

Regensburg Cathedral (Dom St. Peter)

An awe-inspiring Gothic cathedral with towering spires, intricate stained glass, and an interior that echoes the grandeur of medieval craftsmanship.

The Old Town & Historic Sausage Kitchen

The historic center of Regensburg is filled with colorful buildings and lively squares. Don't miss the Historic Sausage Kitchen, a restaurant that has been serving sausages for over 500 years!

Insider Tip: Walk along the Danube River at sunset for a picturesque view of the city's skyline.

Regensburg

Franconian Wine Country: A Hidden Treasure

The Franconian wine region, located just outside Nuremberg, is a paradise for wine lovers. Unlike Bavaria's beer-dominated culture, this region is known for its dry, mineral-rich white wines, especially Silvaner.

Würzburg & The Residenz Palace

Start your wine journey in Würzburg, home to the Residenz, an opulent Baroque palace with breathtaking frescoes and an awe-inspiring staircase designed by Balthasar Neumann.

The Vineyards of Volkach & Sommerach

These picturesque vineyard towns offer intimate wine-tasting experiences. Visit a local Weinstube (wine tavern) and enjoy Franconian specialties paired with exceptional local wines.

The Bocksbeutel Bottle – A Franconian Tradition

You'll notice that Franconian wines come in a distinctively shaped round bottle called a Bocksbeutel. This unique design is legally protected and symbolizes the high quality of Franconian wines.

Insider Tip

Visit during the wine festivals in summer and early autumn for an unforgettable cultural experience.

Dachau Concentration Camp Memorial Site

A visit to the Dachau Concentration Camp Memorial Site is a sobering and essential experience for those seeking to understand Germany's history during World War II.

The Entrance & Jourhaus Gate

The infamous gate bearing the words "Arbeit macht frei" ("Work sets you free") stands as a stark reminder of the atrocities committed here.

The Barracks & Prison Cells

Step inside the reconstructed barracks to see the cramped living conditions of the prisoners. The original prison cells remain intact, offering a harrowing glimpse into the past.

The Memorial Site & Museum

The museum houses artifacts, photographs, and testimonies that chronicle the harrowing history of Dachau. Outside, memorials erected by different nations stand as a tribute to the victims.

Insider Tip: Allow at least half a day to explore the site in its entirety, and take a moment to reflect on the religious memorials scattered throughout the camp.

Final Thoughts

Each of these day trips offers a unique perspective on Bavaria's history, culture, and natural beauty. Whether you're wandering through Rothenburg's medieval streets, sampling Franconian wines, or reflecting at Dachau, you'll find that these excursions add depth and richness to your journey through Nuremberg and beyond.

Insider Tip

Purchase a Bavaria Ticket (Bayern Ticket) for unlimited regional train travel for the day—it's an economical way to explore multiple destinations from Nuremberg!

Chapter 13

Nuremberg for Different Types of Travelers

Whether you're planning a romantic retreat, going on a single trip, or looking for unusual experiences with friends or family, Nuremberg has something to offer all types of tourists. Everyone may find something exceptional in Nuremberg, from its rich history to its lively cultural offers and quaint hidden nooks. This chapter examines how various tourists might maximize their time in this intriguing Bavarian city.

Solo Travelers: Safety & Must-Know Tips

Traveling solo in Nuremberg is a rewarding experience, allowing you to explore the city at your own pace while diving deep into its medieval charm, vibrant arts scene, and delicious culinary offerings. Safety is a key concern for solo travelers, but Nuremberg is known for being a welcoming and secure destination.

Safe & Welcoming Environment

Nuremberg consistently ranks as one of Germany's safest cities. The Old Town is well-lit and patrolled, and public transport is reliable. As a solo traveler, it's always advisable to stay aware of your surroundings, especially in less crowded areas at night, but overall, you can enjoy the city with ease.

Best Solo Activities in Nuremberg

- **Exploring the Old Town (Altstadt):** Take a self-guided tour of Hauptmarkt, Schöner Brunnen, and the medieval alleyways.

- **Museums & Cultural Sites:** Dive into history at the Germanisches Nationalmuseum or visit the haunting yet insightful Memorium Nuremberg Trials.

- **Local Cafés & Beer Gardens:** Grab a book and enjoy the atmosphere at Café Bar Katz or experience the communal tables at Hausbrauerei Altstadthof.

- **Day Trips:** Visit the charming town of Bamberg, famous for its smoked beer and half-timbered houses.

Public Transport & Navigation

The city's trams and buses make it easy to get around. A **Nürnberg Card** is a great investment, offering unlimited public transport and free entry to major attractions.

Romantic Getaways for Couples

Nuremberg's fairy-tale ambiance, with its historic castles, scenic river views, and cozy restaurants, makes it an ideal destination for couples seeking a romantic escape.

Enchanting Strolls & Scenic Spots

- **Hand-in-Hand Through the Castle District:** The walk up to Nuremberg Castle rewards couples with breathtaking panoramic views over the city. The castle courtyard at sunset is particularly magical.

- **Pegnitz River & Henkersteg Bridge:** A romantic evening stroll along the Pegnitz River, passing through Henkersteg, is a must for lovebirds. The illuminated reflections on the water create an unforgettable atmosphere.

- **Tiergärtnertorplatz:** A lively yet intimate square perfect for sipping wine while watching the world go by.

Candlelit Dinners & Cozy Eateries

- **Essigbrätlein:** This Michelin-starred gem offers an unforgettable fine dining experience for couples who appreciate gourmet cuisine.

- **Albrecht-Dürer-Stube:** Tucked away in a charming half-timbered house, this restaurant serves traditional Franconian dishes in a warm, intimate setting.

- **Romantic Wine Cellars:** Enjoy local Franconian wines in the historic wine cellars of

Weinstadel, a former medieval hospital turned dining haven.

Couple-Friendly Activities

- **Relaxing Spa Experiences:** The Kristall Palm Beach Thermal Spa offers couples wellness treatments, thermal pools, and sauna experiences.

- **Horse-Drawn Carriage Rides:** Experience a ride through the Old Town's cobbled streets for a classic romantic moment.

- **Christmas Market Magic:** If visiting in winter, the Christkindlesmarkt is an enchanting setting for couples to sip glühwein and soak in the festive spirit.

Family-Friendly Activities & Attractions in Nuremberg

Nuremberg Zoo – A Wildlife Adventure

One of the best places to take children in Nuremberg is the **Tiergarten Nürnberg (Nuremberg Zoo)**, one of the largest and most beautiful zoos in Europe. Located in a lush, forested area, this zoo is home to more than 300 species, including elephants, tigers, dolphins, and polar bears.

- **Dolphin Lagoon & Manatee House** – One of the standout features of the zoo is the Dolphin Lagoon, where families can watch dolphins perform and learn about marine conservation. The adjacent Manatee House provides a rare chance to see these gentle sea creatures up close.

- **Children's Farm** – Kids can interact with friendly farm animals such as goats, sheep, and rabbits, making for a delightful hands-on experience.

- **Playgrounds & Picnic Areas** – Scattered throughout the zoo are fantastic playgrounds and shaded picnic spots, perfect for a relaxing family break.

Tip: Arrive early in the morning when the animals are most active, and bring a packed lunch to enjoy in the picnic area.

The Toy Museum – A Magical Journey Through Childhood

Nuremberg has a deep-rooted history in toy-making, making the **Spielzeugmuseum (Toy Museum)** a must-visit for families. This museum takes visitors on a fascinating journey through the history of toys, from ancient wooden dolls to modern-day playthings.

- **Historic Toy Collections** – See centuries-old toys, including dollhouses, model trains, and handcrafted tin soldiers.

- **Hands-On Play Areas** – Kids can play with a variety of classic and modern toys, making the visit interactive and engaging.

- **Outdoor Garden Play Area** – During warmer months, the museum's outdoor garden transforms into a fun play space with traditional games and activities.

Tip: Visit during weekdays to avoid crowds and ensure your children get the most out of the interactive exhibits.

Playmobil FunPark – Where Imagination Comes to Life

For a day filled with adventure and creativity, head to **Playmobil FunPark**, located just outside of Nuremberg in Zirndorf. Unlike traditional amusement parks with rides, this park is designed as a massive interactive playground where children can explore different themed worlds.

- **Pirate Ship Adventure** – Kids can climb aboard a giant pirate ship, complete with slides and water play features.

- **Knights' Castle & Fairy Tale Land** – Let your little ones become knights, kings, and princesses as they explore medieval castles and enchanting fairy tale settings.

- **Farm and Construction Zone** – Children can interact with lifelike farm animals and operate toy construction equipment in a fun, hands-on environment.

Tip: The park is best suited for children between ages 3 and 10. Be sure to bring a change of clothes, as many attractions involve water play.

Nuremberg Castle – A Fairytale Experience

Kids fascinated by knights and castles will love exploring the **Kaiserburg (Imperial Castle of Nuremberg)**, one of the city's most iconic landmarks. This medieval fortress offers breathtaking views of the city and plenty of exciting spaces for young adventurers to explore.

- **Knight's Hall & Watchtower** – Learn about medieval weapons, armor, and castle life while climbing to the top of the watchtower for panoramic views.

- **Underground Secret Passageways** – Guided tours of the castle's underground tunnels offer an exciting adventure into Nuremberg's past.

- **Castle Gardens** – Let the kids run free in the beautifully maintained gardens, perfect for a mid-day break.

Tip: The castle is best explored in the morning to avoid crowds. Consider taking a guided family-friendly tour for a more engaging experience.

The German Railway Museum – A Journey Through Time

For train-loving kids (and adults!), the **Deutsches Bahn Museum (German Railway Museum)** is a fantastic stop. This museum showcases the history of rail transport in Germany, featuring historic steam locomotives, modern high-speed trains, and interactive exhibits.

- **Historic Train Exhibits** – Explore real locomotives from different periods, including a royal train carriage used by German emperors.

- **Kids' Play Area** – A dedicated play section allows children to operate miniature trains and explore railway-themed activities.

- **Simulator Experience** – Older kids can try their hand at driving a virtual train through a fun and educational simulator.

Tip: Look for special seasonal events, such as model train exhibitions and interactive workshops, which make the experience even more exciting.

Nuremberg's Beautiful Parks & Outdoor Spaces

When the weather is nice, Nuremberg offers fantastic parks where families can relax and enjoy outdoor activities.

- **Luitpoldhain Park** – A large, scenic park perfect for picnics, cycling, and playing in open green spaces.

- **Wöhrder See** – This lakeside park is ideal for families, offering walking trails, paddle boat rentals, and a children's water play area.

- **Marienberg Park** – A quieter alternative, this park features well-maintained playgrounds and shaded areas for a peaceful afternoon with kids.

Tip: Bring a frisbee, football, or kite to make the most of Nuremberg's outdoor spaces while keeping the kids entertained.

Final Thoughts

Nuremberg is a city that caters exceptionally well to families, offering a perfect blend of history, fun attractions, and engaging experiences for children of all ages. From medieval castles and immersive museums to expansive zoos and thrilling play parks, there's no shortage of memorable activities for parents and kids alike. By planning and choosing family-friendly spots, you're sure to create an unforgettable experience for the whole family.

Budget Travel: Saving Money While Enjoying Nuremberg

Traveling on a budget doesn't mean compromising on experiences. Nuremberg offers a variety of affordable attractions, free activities, and budget-friendly dining spots that allow visitors to soak in the city's rich history and vibrant culture without breaking the bank.

Affordable Accommodation Options

- **Hostels & Budget Hotels**: Nuremberg has several clean and comfortable hostels like Five

Reasons Hotel & Hostel and A&O Nürnberg Hauptbahnhof, offering dorm beds and budget-friendly private rooms.

- **Guesthouses & Pension Houses**: For a cozy and affordable stay, consider Pension Im Bett or Hotel Continental, both providing comfortable accommodations at reasonable rates.

- **Airbnb & Budget Apartments**: Renting a private room or an entire apartment can be cost-effective for longer stays, especially if you're traveling with a group.

Free & Low-Cost Attractions

- **Kaiserburg Castle Grounds**: While entry to the main castle has a fee, the castle grounds and gardens offer fantastic panoramic views of the city—completely free.

- **Stroll Through the Altstadt (Old Town)**: Walking through Nuremberg's Old Town is like stepping back in time. Enjoy historic landmarks like Schöner Brunnen and the medieval city walls without spending a dime.

- **Free Museums on Specific Days**: Many of Nuremberg's museums, like the Germanisches Nationalmuseum and the Albrecht Dürer House, offer free entry on the first Sunday of every month.

- **Handwerkerhof**: This charming artisan village is free to explore, where you can watch craftsmen at work and soak in the medieval ambiance.

Cheap Eats & Budget Dining

- **Bratwurst Stands**: A visit to Nuremberg isn't complete without trying the famous Nürnberger Rostbratwurst. Grab a delicious bratwurst at Bratwursthäusle or Rösterei Kaffee for an affordable yet authentic meal.

- **Supermarkets & Bakeries**: Budget travelers can pick up fresh pretzels, sandwiches, and pastries from local bakeries like Der Beck, or shop for picnic ingredients at Edeka or Aldi.

- **Student Cafeterias & Imbiss Stalls**: University cafeterias offer affordable meals, and small snack stalls serve local delicacies at lower prices than restaurants.

Budget-Friendly Transportation

- **Nuremberg Card**: A must for budget travelers, this card provides free public transport and entry to major attractions for 48 hours at an affordable price.

- **Walking & Biking**: Nuremberg is very walkable, and renting a bike is an inexpensive way to explore the city while staying active.

- **Day Pass for Public Transport**: If you plan to travel around the city, get a TagesTicket (Day Ticket) to save on multiple rides.

Best Time to Visit for Budget Travelers

- Traveling during the off-season (January to March) can save you money on accommodations and attractions, while still enjoying Nuremberg's beautiful winter scenery.

Luxury Travel: Exclusive Experiences

For those seeking indulgence, Nuremberg offers a wealth of high-end experiences, from lavish accommodations and Michelin-starred dining to exclusive tours and spa retreats.

High-End Accommodation

- **Le Méridien Grand Hotel Nürnberg**: A five-star hotel offering opulent rooms with a blend of modern luxury and historic charm.

- **Hotel Drei Raben**: A boutique luxury hotel where each room tells a unique story about Nuremberg's history.

- **Sheraton Carlton Hotel**: Boasting a rooftop spa, luxurious suites, and gourmet dining, this is the perfect retreat for luxury travelers.

Fine Dining & Michelin-Starred Restaurants

- **Essigbrätlein**: A Michelin-starred restaurant offering innovative takes on Franconian cuisine with locally sourced ingredients.

- **Restaurant Wonka**: Known for its exquisite tasting menus and impeccable service.

- **C'era Una Volta**: An exclusive Italian fine dining experience in the heart of Nuremberg.

Exclusive Cultural & Historical Experiences

- **Private Guided Tours**: Book a personal tour of Nuremberg Castle, Albrecht Dürer's House, or even a WWII historical tour tailored to your interests.

- **VIP Access to Concerts & Opera**: Enjoy a night at the Nuremberg State Theatre or book a VIP box at the Meistersingerhalle for an unparalleled cultural experience.

- **Behind-the-Scenes Brewery Tours**: Get an exclusive look at how traditional Bavarian beer is brewed with special tasting sessions.

Luxury Shopping & Unique Finds

- **Breuninger Nürnberg**: A high-end department store featuring luxury fashion brands.

- **Handmade Crafts & Designer Boutiques**: Visit independent designers and high-end craft shops in the Old Town for one-of-a-kind souvenirs.

- **Exclusive Christmas Market Experience**: During the famous Christkindlesmarkt, book a private tour to enjoy the market before the crowds arrive.

Relaxation & Wellness

- **High-End Spa Retreats**: Visit Adina Spa or the Carlton Spa for world-class massages, saunas, and wellness treatments.

- **Private River Cruises**: Enjoy a romantic private cruise along the Pegnitz River, complete with fine dining and champagne.

- **Luxury Car Rentals**: Experience Nuremberg in style with a luxury vehicle rental, perfect for a road trip to nearby Bavarian castles.

Best Time to Visit for Luxury Travelers

- December is perfect for experiencing the world-famous Christmas Market in style, while spring and autumn offer mild weather and exclusive seasonal events.

Insider Tip

For an extra special evening, book a table at **Das Steichele**, a family-run restaurant with a cozy, candlelit ambiance serving some of the best regional dishes and wines in Nuremberg. Arrive early and request a seat near the fireplace for a truly romantic setting.

If you're visiting in December, don't miss the **Nuremberg Christkindlesmarkt**, one of the most famous Christmas markets in the world. The **Children's Christmas Market (Kinderweihnacht)** offers carousel rides, cookie decorating workshops, and puppet shows, making it a magical experience for young visitors.

Chapter 14

Suggested Itineraries for Every Traveler

Rich in culture and history, Nuremberg offers a unique fusion of medieval and contemporary attractions. Planning will guarantee that you get the most out of your trip, whether you have one day to explore or three days to fully experience its delights. Two carefully planned itineraries are offered below to accommodate two distinct traveler types: those with busy schedules and those who want to explore Nuremberg more leisurely and thoroughly.

One-Day Express Tour of Nuremberg

If you only have a day in Nuremberg, every moment counts. This itinerary is designed to give you an immersive experience covering the city's most iconic highlights, offering a perfect mix of history, culture, and culinary delights.

Morning: Exploring Nuremberg's Old Town

Start your day early at **Nuremberg Castle (Kaiserburg)**, the city's most iconic landmark. This impressive medieval fortress provides panoramic views of the entire city. Walk through its centuries-old courtyards, explore the Imperial Chapel, and visit the Deep Well, a 50-meter-deep structure dating back to the Middle Ages.

Next, head downhill towards the **Albrecht Dürer House**, a beautifully preserved 15th-century timber-framed house that once belonged to Germany's most famous Renaissance artist. The museum inside showcases his original works and a glimpse into his life and workshop.

From here, take a stroll down **Weißgerbergasse**, one of Nuremberg's most picturesque streets, lined with half-timbered houses and boutique shops. This is a perfect spot for quick photographs and a traditional Franconian breakfast at one of the cozy cafés.

Midday: Dive into History at the Nazi Documentation Center

A short tram ride will take you to the **Documentation Center Nazi Party Rally Grounds**, one of the most significant sites in Nuremberg's modern history. The museum provides an insightful and sobering look into the events leading to World War II and the role Nuremberg played during that era. Allocate at least an hour here for an in-depth visit.

Afternoon: Culinary and Market Square Experience

Return to the heart of the city and visit the Hauptmarkt (Main Market Square), where you'll find the stunning Schöner Brunnen (Beautiful Fountain) and the historic Frauenkirche (Church of Our Lady). Depending on the season, you might witness the bustling Christmas Market or enjoy fresh produce from local vendors.

For lunch, indulge in **Nuremberg's famous Rostbratwurst** at **Bratwursthäusle**, a historic sausage kitchen serving grilled Franconian sausages with sauerkraut and mustard.

Evening: A Relaxing Stroll and Farewell to Nuremberg

Wrap up your day with a serene walk along the **Pegnitz River** and visit the **Handwerkerhof**, a charming medieval-style artisan courtyard. If time permits, enjoy a glass of local Franconian wine or a pint of Tucher beer at a nearby tavern before bidding farewell to Nuremberg.

A 3-Day Nuremberg Itinerary

For travelers with more time, a three-day itinerary allows for a deeper dive into Nuremberg's cultural scene, historical sites, and surrounding areas.

Day 1: Classic Nuremberg Highlights

Follow the One-Day Express Tour for your first day, covering the Old Town, Nuremberg Castle, Albrecht Dürer House, the Nazi Documentation Center, and the vibrant Hauptmarkt.

Day 2: Museums and Hidden Gems

Start with a visit to the **Germanisches Nationalmuseum**, Germany's largest museum of cultural history. It houses extensive collections of medieval art, musical instruments, and historical artifacts.

Next, explore the **Toy Museum (Spielzeugmuseum)**, an enchanting space showcasing Nuremberg's legacy as a global toy manufacturing hub.

For lunch, head to the **Weinstadel**, a charming riverside restaurant serving Franconian delicacies.

In the afternoon, visit the **Memorium Nuremberg Trials** at the Palace of Justice, the historic courtroom where Nazi war criminals were tried after World War II.

As the sun sets, enjoy a tranquil moment at the **Johannisfriedhof Cemetery**, where Albrecht Dürer is buried. The well-maintained flower beds and artistic gravestones offer a peaceful ambiance.

Day 3: Day Trip & Local Experience

For your final day, take a short train ride to **Bamberg**, a UNESCO World Heritage town known as the "Little

Venice of Bavaria." Explore its medieval streets, visit the Bamberg Cathedral, and admire the half-timbered Altes Rathaus built in the middle of the river.

Return to Nuremberg in the afternoon and take a break at a local **beer garden**, such as **Hexenhäusle**, for a refreshing Franconian beer experience.

In the evening, conclude your Nuremberg journey with a relaxing boat ride along the Pegnitz River or a cultural performance at the **Staatstheater Nürnberg**.

5-Day Itinerary with Excursions

Day 1: Historic Nuremberg – A Walk Through Time

Start your journey by stepping into the past as you explore the Old Town, a place where medieval charm and wartime history intertwine seamlessly.

- **Nuremberg Castle (Kaiserburg)** – Begin your day at the iconic Nuremberg Castle. Walk along the fortified walls for panoramic city views and explore the deep wells and historical exhibits inside.

- **Albrecht Dürer's House** – A short stroll downhill takes you to the home of Germany's Renaissance master, Albrecht Dürer. Gain insight into his artistic process and the impact of his works.

- **Weißgerbergasse** – Wander through this picturesque street with half-timbered houses, once home to tanners and artisans.

- **St. Sebaldus Church & Hauptmarkt** – Visit one of the oldest churches in Nuremberg before arriving at Hauptmarkt, where the legendary Schöner Brunnen (Beautiful Fountain) stands.

- **Nuremberg's Underground Tunnels** – End the day with a fascinating tour through medieval beer cellars and World War II bunkers beneath the city.

Day 2: A Deep Dive into History

- **Documentation Center Nazi Party Rally Grounds** – Delve into the darkest chapter of Nuremberg's history by exploring this powerful museum.

- **Memorium Nuremberg Trials** – Stand in the very room where Nazi leaders were held accountable for their crimes.

- **Germanisches Nationalmuseum** – Explore Germany's largest cultural history museum, housing everything from medieval artifacts to modern art.

- **Handwerkerhof** – Unwind in this charming medieval craftsmen's courtyard, where you can shop for handmade souvenirs and taste traditional Franconian delicacies.

Day 3: Nuremberg's Art, Science & Innovation

- **DB Museum (German Railway Museum)** – A must-visit for train enthusiasts, showcasing Germany's railway history.

- **Toy Museum (Spielzeugmuseum)** – Rediscover childhood nostalgia with one of the most impressive toy collections in Europe.

- **Zoological Garden (Tiergarten Nürnberg)** – Spend the afternoon visiting one of Germany's most scenic zoos.
- **Dinner at a Traditional Biergarten** – Enjoy an authentic Franconian meal with locally brewed beer in a cozy outdoor setting.

Day 4: Day Trip to Rothenburg ob der Tauber

- **Travel by Train or Car** – Less than two hours away, Rothenburg is the quintessential medieval town.
- **Walk the City Walls** – Admire the well-preserved fortifications and towers surrounding the town.
- **Marktplatz & Christmas Museum** – Explore the town square and visit the world-famous Käthe Wohlfahrt Christmas store.
- **Plönlein & Castle Gardens** – Capture picture-perfect moments at these iconic spots.
- **Return to Nuremberg for Dinner** – Relish a Franconian feast at a local restaurant.

Day 5: Relaxing and Hidden Gems

- **Franconian Wine Tasting in a Local Vineyard** – Discover the region's underrated yet exquisite wines.

- **Hesperidengärten (Hesperides Gardens)** – Stroll through these elegant Baroque gardens.

- **St. Johannis Cemetery** – Visit the beautifully landscaped cemetery, the resting place of Albrecht Dürer.

- **Dinner Cruise on the Pegnitz River** – End your Nuremberg adventure with a scenic river cruise.

The Ultimate Week-Long Adventure

For those with more time, extend your Nuremberg journey to seven days with these additional excursions and experiences:

Day 6: Bamberg – The Little Venice of Bavaria

- **Bamberg Old Town** – A UNESCO World Heritage Site with stunning medieval architecture.

- **Altes Rathaus (Old Town Hall)** – A picturesque half-timbered building standing in the middle of the Regnitz River.

- **Bamberg Cathedral & Rose Garden** – Visit the impressive cathedral before relaxing in the serene rose garden.

- **Schlenkerla Brewery** – Sample Bamberg's famous smoked beer.

Day 7: A Scenic Finale – Regensburg or Franconian Switzerland

Option 1: Regensburg

- Visit the **Stone Bridge**, **Regensburg Cathedral**, and the **Historic Sausage Kitchen** for a final taste of Bavarian culture.

Option 2: Franconian Switzerland

- Discover a landscape of rolling hills, dramatic rock formations, and charming villages.

- Explore stalactite caves, and medieval castles, and hike through the breathtaking scenery.

Insider Tip: If you visit Nuremberg during December, extend your itinerary to include the world-famous **Christkindlesmarkt**, one of Europe's oldest and most magical Christmas markets. The festive atmosphere, traditional wooden stalls, and delicious gingerbread make it an unforgettable experience.

For an unforgettable experience, visit Nuremberg during the Christmas season. The **Christkindlesmarkt**, one of the most famous Christmas markets in the world, transforms the city into a winter wonderland filled with twinkling lights, festive stalls, and the sweet aroma of gingerbread.

Chapter 15

Hidden Gems & Insider Tips in Nuremberg

One of Germany's most fascinating cities is Nuremberg, with its ancient town, half-timbered houses, and diverse cultural heritage. The city is home to numerous lesser-known gems that are just waiting to be discovered, even while famous sites like Christkindlesmarkt and the Imperial Castle (Kaiserburg) are must-see attractions. By bringing you off the typical tourist route, these hidden jewels provide a more personal, genuine experience of Nuremberg. You will find amazing vistas, hidden locations, underappreciated museums, and unique experiences that only locals are aware of.

In this chapter, we'll unveil some of **Nuremberg's best-kept secrets**, from secluded beer gardens and charming cobblestone alleys to underground labyrinths and offbeat cultural experiences. Whether you're a history buff, a foodie, or a curious explorer, these hidden gems will make your visit to Nuremberg truly special.

Secret Spots Only Locals Know

Johannisfriedhof – Nuremberg's Most Beautiful Cemetery

Johannisfriedhof

While tourists flock to the city's bustling streets, few take the time to visit the serene **Johannisfriedhof (St. John's Cemetery)**, a hidden oasis of calm. This historic burial ground, dating back to the 16th century, is known for its unique gravestones made of red sandstone and its famous residents, including the renowned artist **Albrecht Dürer** and sculptor **Veit Stoss**.

- **Why Visit?** Stroll among centuries-old tombstones, many adorned with intricate carvings and inscriptions.

- **Insider Tip:** Visit at sunset when the golden light bathes the cemetery in a soft, ethereal glow—perfect for photographers and history lovers alike.

Kettensteg – The Oldest Iron Chain Bridge in Germany

While everyone rushes to the **Heilig-Geist-Spital** for a photo, **Kettensteg** remains a peaceful alternative with just as much charm. Built in **1824**, this suspension bridge is Germany's oldest surviving iron chain bridge.

- **Why Visit?** Provides a **unique, Instagram-worthy view** of the Pegnitz River and Nuremberg's medieval architecture.

- **Insider Tip:** For the best experience, visit in the early morning when the bridge is quiet and the soft light bathes the city in golden hues.

Weißgerbergasse – The Most Picturesque Street in Nuremberg

Hidden away from the bustling main squares, **Weißgerbergasse** is a stunning medieval street lined with **pastel-colored half-timbered houses**. Once home to Nuremberg's tanners, today it's an **underrated but breathtaking** gem.

- **Why Visit?** One of the best-preserved historical streets in the city with charming cafés, local artisan shops, and an authentic medieval atmosphere.

- **Insider Tip:** Visit at sunrise or dusk for the most magical lighting, and stop by **Café Wanderer** for a quiet coffee with a view of Albrecht Dürer's house.

Underrated Parks & Gardens for a Tranquil Escape

Hesperidengärten – The Hidden Baroque Garden

Just a short walk from the bustling city center, the **Hesperidengärten (Hesperides Gardens)** offers a peaceful retreat away from the tourist crowds.

- **Secret Beauty:** This Baroque-style garden is adorned with **stone statues, fountains, and meticulously sculpted hedges**.

- **Ideal for a Stroll or a Picnic:** Bring a book, soak in the serene atmosphere, and admire the classic **Renaissance-style design**.

- **Insider Tip:** Visit in the early evening when the golden glow of the sunset bathes the garden, offering a picture-perfect setting.

Volkspark Marienberg – A Local's Favorite Getaway

Unlike the often-crowded parks near the Old Town, **Volkspark Marienberg** is a beloved **locals-only retreat** perfect for leisurely walks, jogging, or a peaceful afternoon surrounded by nature.

- **Why Visit?** Spanning **more than 100 hectares**, this park has **lush green spaces, a small lake, and scenic walking paths**.

- **Ideal for Outdoor Enthusiasts:** Great for jogging, picnicking, or enjoying a relaxed afternoon in nature.

- **Fun for Families:** Features include a playground, mini-golf course, and bird-watching spots.

Where to Find the Best Views of Nuremberg

Sinwell Tower – Nuremberg's Most Iconic View

One of the best ways to see the city is from **Sinwell Tower**, part of the **Imperial Castle (Kaiserburg)**.

- **Breathtaking Panoramic Views:** Get a **bird's-eye view of the city** and see the picturesque half-timbered houses, red rooftops, and rolling countryside.

- **Historical Significance:** Built in the **13th century**, the tower is a piece of medieval engineering marvel.

- **Insider Tip:** Visit around sunset to watch the cityscape bathe in golden light for the most magical view.

Altstadt Viewpoints – Spectacular Perspectives

For those seeking a **quieter viewpoint**, the **Kettensteg** is a historic iron footbridge providing stunning views of the Old Town and the Pegnitz River.

Alternatively, climb to **Burgberg** for an elevated panorama of Nuremberg's rooftops.

- **Best Sunset Spot: Burgberg Gardens**, near the castle, offers a tranquil place to watch the sunset.

- **Alternative City View:** Head to **Luitpoldhain Park**, where the elevated hill presents a unique perspective of the city skyline.

Unusual Experiences & Off-the-Beaten-Path Adventures

The Underground World of Felsengänge

Nuremberg is famous for its underground tunnels, with the **Historische Felsengänge** being one of the most exciting attractions.

- **Why Visit?** These medieval rock-cut cellars were originally used for fermenting and storing **Nuremberg's world-famous beer**.

- **World War II Connection:** The tunnels became air raid shelters, protecting thousands of citizens during Allied bombings.

- **Insider Tip:** Join a guided tour to explore hidden **labyrinthine passages** and learn about their history.

Experience a Franconian Beer Hike

For a truly offbeat experience, embark on the famous **Five-Seidla-Steig**, a scenic trail linking several local breweries.

- **Best Beer Stops:** Includes classic Franconian breweries like **Brauerei Neder** and **Brauerei Roppelt**.

- **Scenic Route:** Walk past picturesque villages, half-timbered houses, and rolling hills.

- **Tip:** Try the locally brewed **Kellerbier**, unfiltered and fresh from the tap for the best experience.

Insider Tip: To experience the Christmas magic without the peak-hour crowds at the

Christkindlesmarkt, visit on a weekday in the late afternoon. The market is busiest in the evenings, especially on weekends, so arrive early to enjoy the decorations and grab a spot for the famous **Nuremberg sausages** before the lines get long. For an extra special experience, hop on a horse-drawn **Christmas carriage ride** through the Old Town—it's like stepping into a fairytale.

Chapter 16

Sustainable & Responsible Travel in Nuremberg

The historic and culturally rich city of Nuremberg is also making great progress in the direction of sustainability. You may maximize your enjoyment as a visitor while minimizing your environmental impact by making eco-friendly decisions. This chapter will teach you how to enjoy Nuremberg while honoring the city's ecology and community, from booking lodging at eco-friendly establishments to patronizing neighborhood shops and taking green transportation.

Eco-Friendly Hotels and Stays – Where to Stay Sustainably

Sustainability in hospitality is becoming a priority in Nuremberg, with many hotels adopting eco-friendly practices such as renewable energy use, zero-waste policies, and locally sourced food. Whether you prefer boutique stays or large hotels, there are several great options for responsible travelers.

- **Bio Hotel Kunstquartier** – This charming boutique hotel, located in nearby Stein, operates on organic principles, using sustainable building materials, offering organic breakfast, and ensuring low-impact hospitality.

Bio Hotel Kunstquartier

- **Mövenpick Hotel Nürnberg-Airport** – A certified Green Globe hotel that follows strict environmental standards, including energy-efficient lighting, water-saving systems, and sustainable sourcing.

- **Novotel Nürnberg Centre Ville** – Committed to sustainability, this hotel features an energy-efficient building design, eco-friendly amenities, and a strong commitment to waste reduction.

- **Jugendherberge Nürnberg (Nuremberg Youth Hostel)** – Situated in a historic castle, this hostel combines heritage with sustainability, offering energy-efficient accommodations and eco-conscious operations.

How to Choose a Sustainable Stay

- Look for certifications such as Green Key, Green Globe, or EU Ecolabel.

- Opt for hotels that offer reusable amenities, energy-efficient lighting, and water conservation programs.

- Support accommodations that source their food locally and follow fair trade principles.

Supporting Local Businesses – How to Travel Ethically

Responsible tourism is not just about reducing waste but also about uplifting local economies. Nuremberg has a vibrant community of artisans, farmers, and independent business owners who keep the city's traditions alive.

- **Handmade Crafts at Hauptmarkt** – Instead of buying mass-produced souvenirs, visit local artisans at Hauptmarkt to find handmade wooden crafts, traditional Lebkuchen (gingerbread), and local artworks.

- **Independent Cafés & Restaurants** – Rather than dining at chain restaurants opt for locally owned eateries like **Café Mainheim**, which sources ingredients regionally, or **Fränk'ness**, which emphasizes seasonal Franconian cuisine.

- **Organic and Farmers' Markets** – Visit **Bauernmarkt am Hauptmarkt** for organic produce, cheeses, and sustainable goods directly from farmers.

- **Fair Trade Shops** – **Weltladen Nuremberg** sells ethically sourced goods, including textiles, teas, and handicrafts from fair-trade cooperatives worldwide.

Tips for Ethical Shopping

- Choose locally made products instead of imported goods.

- Support small businesses over large corporations.

- Reduce plastic use by carrying reusable shopping bags and containers.

Public Transport & Bike Rentals – Green Ways to Get Around

Nuremberg offers excellent eco-friendly transportation options, making it easy to explore the city sustainably.

- **Trams & Buses** – The **VGN public transport network** runs on low-emission vehicles, offering an efficient way to travel around the city with minimal environmental impact.

- **E-Scooters & Bike Rentals** – Companies like **Nextbike** and **Tier** provide easy-to-use rental bikes and e-scooters, reducing congestion and pollution.

- **Walkable City Center** – Many of Nuremberg's attractions are within walking distance, making it an ideal city to explore on foot.

How to Travel Green in Nuremberg

- Use the **Nürnberg Mobil App** for real-time public transport updates.

- Choose a **day pass** or **week pass** for unlimited travel on trams and buses.

- Rent a **Nextbike** for short distances instead of relying on taxis or ride-shares.

Nuremberg's Green Initiatives – How the City Stays Sustainable

Nuremberg is dedicated to sustainability through various green initiatives that help reduce its carbon footprint and preserve its historical charm.

- **Green Roofs & Urban Gardens** – Several buildings in Nuremberg feature green rooftops that improve air quality and provide insulation.

- **Recycling & Waste Management** – The city has an advanced waste sorting and recycling system, ensuring minimal landfill waste.

- **Sustainable Energy Use** – Many public buildings and transport systems are powered by renewable energy sources.

- **Biodiversity Conservation** – Parks like **Wöhrder See** and **Marienbergpark** focus on preserving local flora and fauna.

How You Can Contribute

- Dispose of waste properly by using the city's recycling bins.

- Choose restaurants and cafes that use compostable packaging.

- Respect nature by staying on designated hiking and biking paths.

Insider Tip: Experience Nuremberg's Eco-Friendly Beer Culture

One of the best ways to enjoy sustainable travel in Nuremberg is through its beer culture. Several breweries, such as **Altstadthof Brewery**, specialize in organic, locally brewed beer made using traditional Franconian methods. Visiting a brewery that values sustainability not only supports local businesses but also gives you an authentic taste of Nuremberg's rich brewing heritage.

Chapter 17

Practical Information for a Stress-Free Trip

Planning a trip to Nuremberg is an exciting endeavor, and ensuring a smooth experience requires attention to key practical details. From safety measures and emergency contacts to currency exchange and payment methods, this chapter provides essential information to help travelers navigate the city with ease. Whether you're a first-time visitor or a seasoned traveler, having these crucial details at your fingertips will enhance your stay and ensure a stress-free journey.

Safety and Health Tips & Emergency Contacts

General Safety in Nuremberg

Nuremberg is generally a very safe city, with a low crime rate compared to other European destinations. However, like any major tourist hub, it is always wise to take precautions:

- **Stay Aware of Your Surroundings** – While violent crime is rare, pickpocketing can occur in crowded areas like Hauptmarkt, train stations, and during festivals.

- **Avoid Unlit Areas at Night** – The Old Town is well-lit and safe, but it's best to stay in well-populated areas after dark.

- **Public Transport Safety** – The U-Bahn (subway), trams, and buses are safe and well-monitored, but always keep an eye on your belongings.

- **Respect Local Laws** – Germany has strict rules regarding public behavior, especially concerning alcohol consumption and noise levels in residential areas.

Emergency Contacts in Nuremberg

Knowing who to call in case of an emergency is essential. Here are the main emergency numbers:

- **Police:** 110 (for all law enforcement-related emergencies)

- **Fire & Ambulance Services:** 112 (for medical emergencies and fire-related incidents)

- **Medical Emergency Service:** 116 117 (for non-life-threatening medical issues outside regular doctor hours)

- **Pharmacies (Apotheke):** Most are open from 9 AM to 6 PM, but an emergency pharmacy service rotates nightly. Check www.aponet.de for the nearest open pharmacy.

- **Tourist Assistance:** The Nuremberg Tourist Information Office can be reached at +49 911 2336-0 for general queries and assistance.

- **Embassies and Consulates:** If you lose your passport or face legal trouble, contact your country's embassy in Berlin or the nearest consulate.

Health and Medical Services

Healthcare in Germany is excellent, with top-notch hospitals and clinics available for tourists if needed.

- **Hospitals with Emergency Departments:** Klinikum Nürnberg (Nuremberg Hospital) is the largest and best-equipped medical facility in the city.

- **Travel Insurance:** It is highly recommended to have travel insurance that covers medical expenses, especially for non-EU travelers.

- **COVID-19 Regulations:** Check Germany's latest health regulations before traveling, as requirements for vaccines, testing, or masks can change.

Currency Exchange & Payment Methods

Currency and Exchange Rates

- **Currency:** The official currency in Nuremberg is the Euro (€).

- **Exchange Rate:** Exchange rates fluctuate, so check reputable financial sources like XE.com before your trip.

- **Where to Exchange Money:** Banks, exchange offices, and even some hotels offer currency exchange, but airports tend to have the worst rates.

- **ATMs:** Widely available throughout the city and usually offer better exchange rates than currency exchange bureaus.

Payment Methods in Nuremberg

- **Credit & Debit Cards:** Visa, MasterCard, and sometimes American Express are accepted in most restaurants, hotels, and shops. However, smaller stores and traditional beer gardens may only accept cash.

- **Contactless Payments:** Apple Pay, Google Pay, and NFC-enabled cards are increasingly popular but not universally accepted, so always carry some cash.

- **Tipping Culture:** Tipping is customary in restaurants (5-10%), taxis (rounding up to the nearest euro), and for hotel staff.

- **Public Transport Tickets:** Purchase tickets at machines or via apps like VGN (Verkehrsverbund Großraum Nürnberg) to avoid last-minute cash needs.

Where to Get Cash

- **ATMs (Geldautomat):** Located at banks, train stations, and shopping centers.

- **Bank Hours:** Typically open Monday-Friday from 9 AM to 4 PM, with some closing for lunch breaks.

- **Avoid Dynamic Currency Conversion:** When using your credit card, always choose to be charged in euros rather than your home currency to get the best exchange rate.

Useful German Phrases for Travelers

Although many people in Nuremberg speak English, especially in tourist areas, knowing a few key German phrases can enrich your experience and earn you friendly smiles from locals. Here are some practical expressions to help you get by:

Greetings & Basic Etiquette

- Hallo! (Hello!)
- Guten Morgen! (Good morning!)
- Guten Abend! (Good evening!)

- Tschüss! (Bye!)
- Bitte (Please)
- Danke (Thank you)
- Entschuldigung (Excuse me/Sorry)

Asking for Directions

- Wo ist...? (Where is...?)
- Wie komme ich zu...? (How do I get to...?)
- Können Sie mir helfen? (Can you help me?)
- Ich habe mich verlaufen. (I'm lost.)

Ordering at Restaurants

- Ich hätte gern... (I would like...)
- Die Speisekarte, bitte. (The menu, please.)
- Kann ich bitte die Rechnung haben? (Can I have the bill, please?)

Shopping & Payments

- Wie viel kostet das? (How much does this cost?)
- Kann ich mit Karte zahlen? (Can I pay by card?)

- Haben Sie das in einer anderen Größe? (Do you have this in another size?)

Transportation & Getting Around

- **Welche Linie fährt nach...?** (Which line goes to...?)
- **Wo ist die nächste Haltestelle?** (Where is the nearest stop?)
- **Wie viel kostet eine Fahrkarte?** (How much is a ticket?)
- **Kann ich ein Tagesticket kaufen?** (Can I buy a day ticket?)
- **Wann fährt der nächste Zug/Bus nach...?** (When does the next train/bus to... leave?)
- **Muss ich umsteigen?** (Do I need to transfer?)

Hotels & Accommodation

- **Haben Sie ein Zimmer frei?** (Do you have a room available?)

- **Ich habe eine Reservierung auf den Namen...** (I have a reservation under the name...)

- **Gibt es kostenloses WLAN?** (Is there free Wi-Fi?)

- **Könnten Sie mir bitte mehr Handtücher bringen?** (Could you bring me more towels, please?)

- **Wann ist der Check-out?** (When is check-out time?)

Emergencies & Medical Assistance

- **Hilfe!** (Help!)

- **Rufen Sie bitte einen Krankenwagen!** (Please call an ambulance!)

- **Ich brauche einen Arzt.** (I need a doctor.)

- **Wo ist die nächste Apotheke?** (Where is the nearest pharmacy?)

- **Ich habe eine Allergie gegen...** (I am allergic to...)

- **Ich habe meine Brieftasche/mein Handy verloren.** (I lost my wallet/phone.)
- **Wo ist die nächste Polizeistation?** (Where is the nearest police station?)

Cultural & Sightseeing

- **Gibt es eine Führung auf Englisch?** (Is there a tour in English?)
- **Wo kann ich Tickets für… kaufen?** (Where can I buy tickets for…?)
- **Wie lange dauert die Tour?** (How long is the tour?)
- **Darf ich hier Fotos machen?** (Can I take photos here?)
- **Gibt es Ermäßigungen für Studenten/Senioren?** (Are there discounts for students/seniors?)

Casual Conversations & Small Talk

- **Wie geht es Ihnen/dir?** (How are you?)
- **Ich komme aus…** (I am from…)

- **Ich bin das erste Mal in Deutschland.** (This is my first time in Germany.)
- **Was empfehlen Sie?** (What do you recommend?)
- **Könnten Sie das bitte wiederholen?** (Could you repeat that, please?)
- **Sprechen Sie Englisch?** (Do you speak English?)

SIM Cards & Wi-Fi Access in Nuremberg

Staying connected while traveling is essential for navigation, translation, and keeping in touch with loved ones. Here's how you can stay online in Nuremberg:

- **Buying a Local SIM Card**
    - The most convenient way to access mobile data in Germany is by purchasing a prepaid SIM card. Major providers

include **Deutsche Telekom (T-Mobile), Vodafone, and O2**.

- o SIM cards are available at **airports, train stations, and electronics stores like MediaMarkt or Saturn.**
- o Plans typically start at **€10-€20 for several gigabytes of data.**
- o Remember that German law requires SIM card registration with an ID, so have your passport ready.

- **Using eSIM Services**
    - o If your phone supports eSIM technology, providers like **Airalo, Holafly, and Truphone** offer digital SIMs, which you can activate instantly without needing a physical card.

- **Free Wi-Fi Spots in Nuremberg**
    - o Nuremberg offers **free Wi-Fi in various public places**, including:

- Nuremberg Main Train Station (**"BayernWLAN"**)
- Hauptmarkt (City Center Square)
- Major museums and libraries
- Many cafes and restaurants (look for signs that say **"WLAN Gratis"** or ask "Haben Sie WLAN?")

   o If you need **unlimited access**, consider renting a **portable Wi-Fi device** from providers like **TravelWiFi** or **Skyroam**.

Best Apps for Navigating the City

To make your time in Nuremberg smooth and stress-free, these apps will be your best companions:

- **Transportation Apps**

   o **Deutsche Bahn (DB Navigator)** – Essential for booking and tracking train schedules in Germany.

- **VGN App** – The official app for Nuremberg's public transport system, providing real-time updates on buses, trams, and subways.
- **Google Maps & Citymapper** – Great for walking directions and transit planning.

- **Language & Translation Apps**
  - **Google Translate** – Offers offline translations and a camera mode to translate signs and menus.
  - **DeepL** – A highly accurate translation app, especially for German.

- **Restaurant & Food Delivery Apps**
  - **TripAdvisor & Yelp** – Discover top-rated restaurants and local specialties.
  - **Wolt & Lieferando** – Popular food delivery services in Nuremberg.

- **Tourism & Cultural Apps**
    - **Visit Nürnberg** – The city's official tourism app with information on attractions, events, and insider tips.
    - **Rick Steves Audio Europe** – Provides engaging audio guides on Nuremberg's historic sites.

Insider Tip

Many smaller businesses in Nuremberg still operate as "cash-preferred" establishments. While digital payment is growing, always keep at least €20-50 in cash to avoid inconvenience, especially when visiting local beer gardens or traditional markets.

If you're staying for an extended period, consider purchasing a **prepaid travel SIM with EU-wide coverage**, like those from **Vodafone CallYa or Telekom Magenta**. This allows you to use data seamlessly in other European cities if you plan to explore beyond Nuremberg.

With these essential travel tools, you'll be well-prepared to navigate Nuremberg efficiently while immersing yourself in the city's rich culture and history.

Map Showing various Emergency Contacts in Nuremberg

Conclusion

Nuremberg is more than just a historical city—it's a living, breathing tapestry of culture, heritage, and modern vibrancy. Whether you're strolling through its medieval streets, savoring its world-famous bratwurst, or uncovering hidden corners known only to locals, every experience in this Bavarian gem leaves an imprint on the soul.

A journey through Nuremberg is a step into a past that has shaped the present, from its imperial castle and half-timbered houses to its rich artistic and culinary traditions. But it's also a city that embraces the future, with sustainable travel initiatives, innovative museums, and a thriving cultural scene that never ceases to surprise.

For those seeking adventure, the lush landscapes surrounding Nuremberg offer endless opportunities for exploration, from scenic hiking trails to serene river cruises. If history is your passion, the city's museums and landmarks provide unparalleled insight into Europe's past. And for food lovers, every bite tells a story—whether it's the smoky aroma of freshly grilled sausages or the sweet indulgence of authentic Lebkuchen.

Perhaps the best part of Nuremberg is its ability to make every visitor feel like a part of its story. The warmth of its people, the energy of its festivals, and the charm of its hidden gems ensure that no two visits are ever the same.

As you plan your journey to this captivating city, remember to explore beyond the well-trodden paths, savor each moment, and embrace the unexpected. Nuremberg is not just a destination—it's an experience waiting to be lived, again and again.

Printed in Dunstable, United Kingdom